KT-546-224

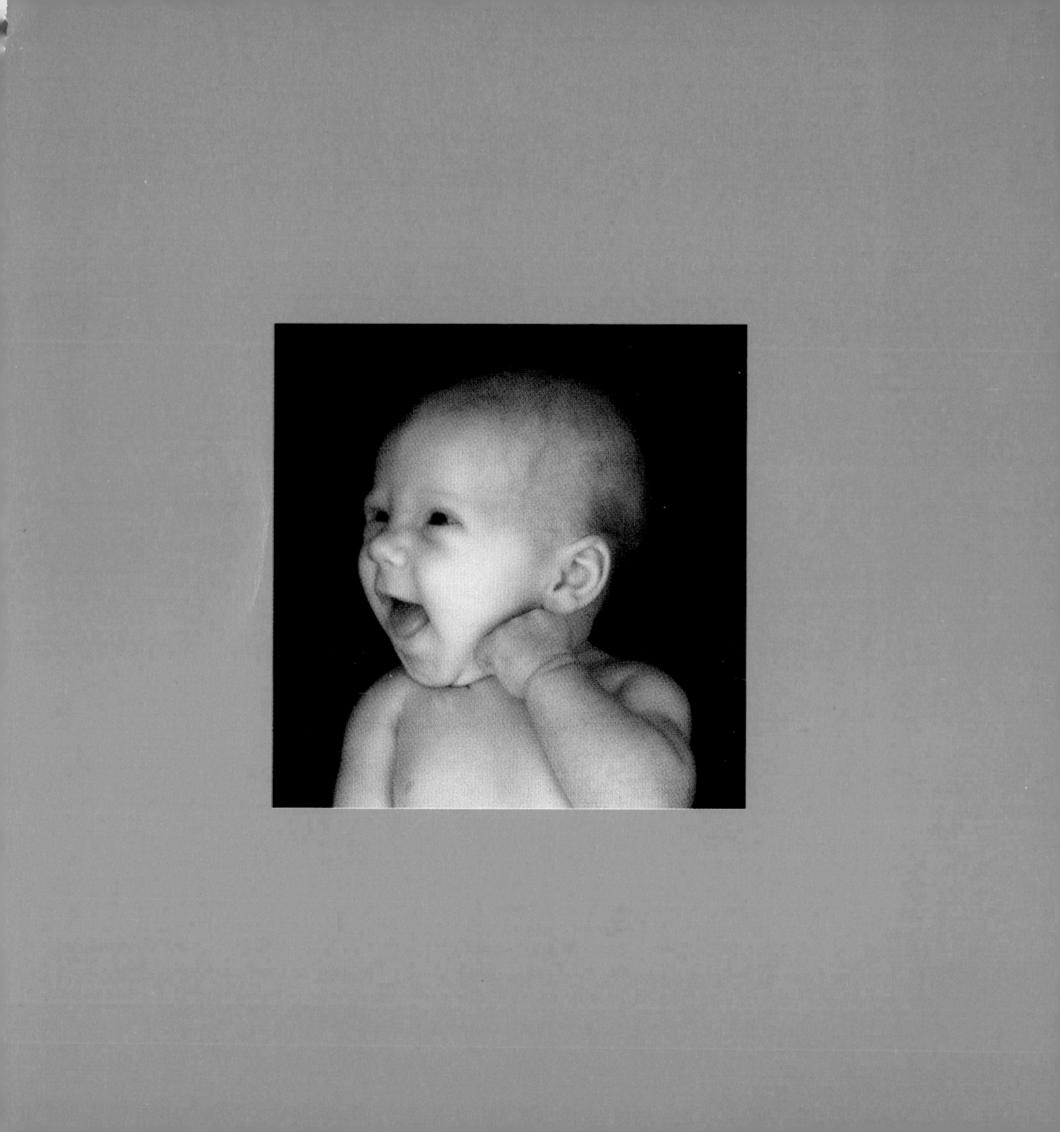

First published in the UK in 2007
by Bailey Hart Publishing
8 Oman Avenue
London NW2 6BG

www.baileyhartpublishing.com

10 9 8 7 6 5 4 3 2 1

ISBN 0-9552843-3-3 978-0-9552843-3-5

Text compilation and Photography by Richard Bailey.
Design and Typography by Hun Wynn
Printed by Toppan Printing Ltd

bhp bailey hart publishing

“ TO BE A *Mum* ”

"

If evolution really works,

how come mothers only have two hands

?

"

- MILTON BERLE

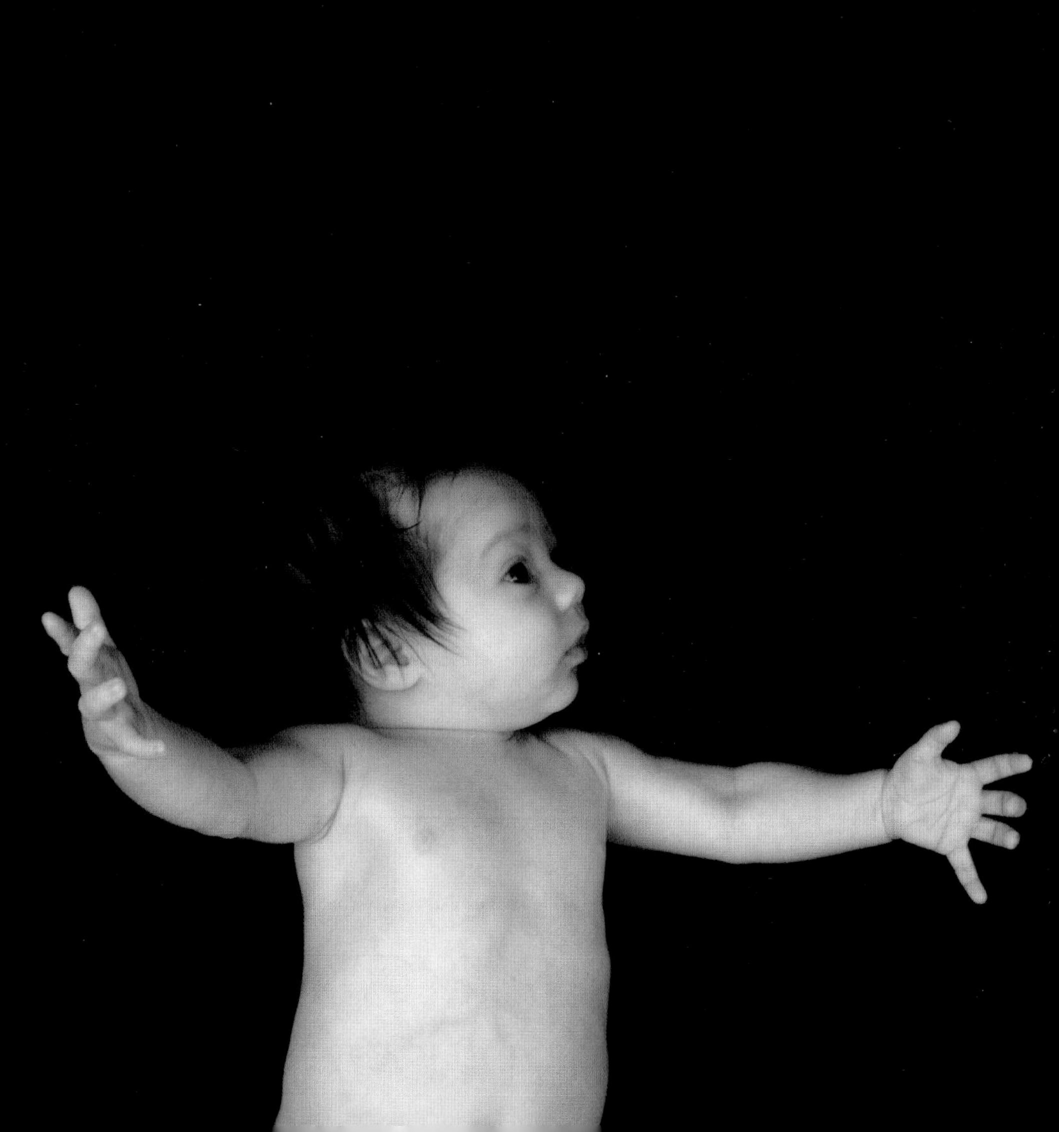

“Laughter

is like changing a baby's diaper.
It doesn't permanently
solve any problems,
but it makes things
more acceptable for a while.”

- UNKNOWN

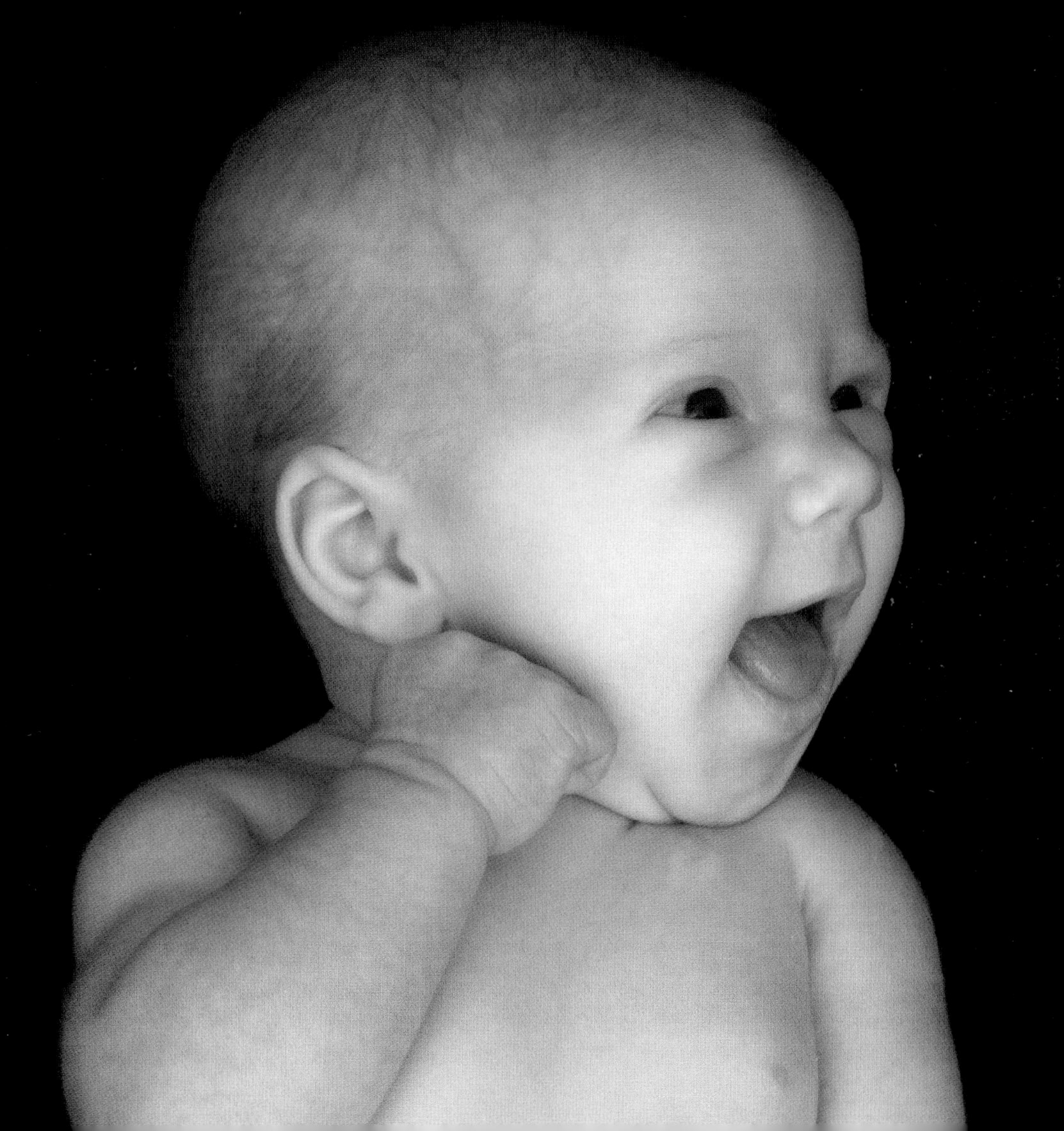

“People who say they sleep like babies
usually don’t have them.”

- LEO J. BURKE

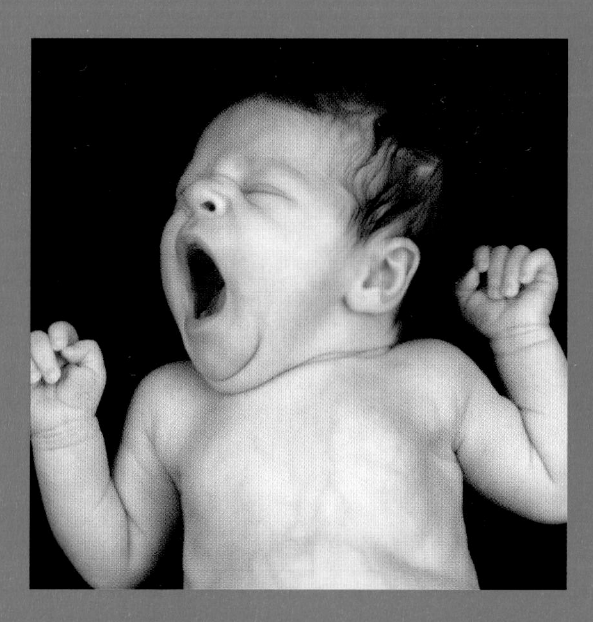

Giving birth

is like

taking your

lower lip

and forcing it

over your head.

- CAROL BURNETT

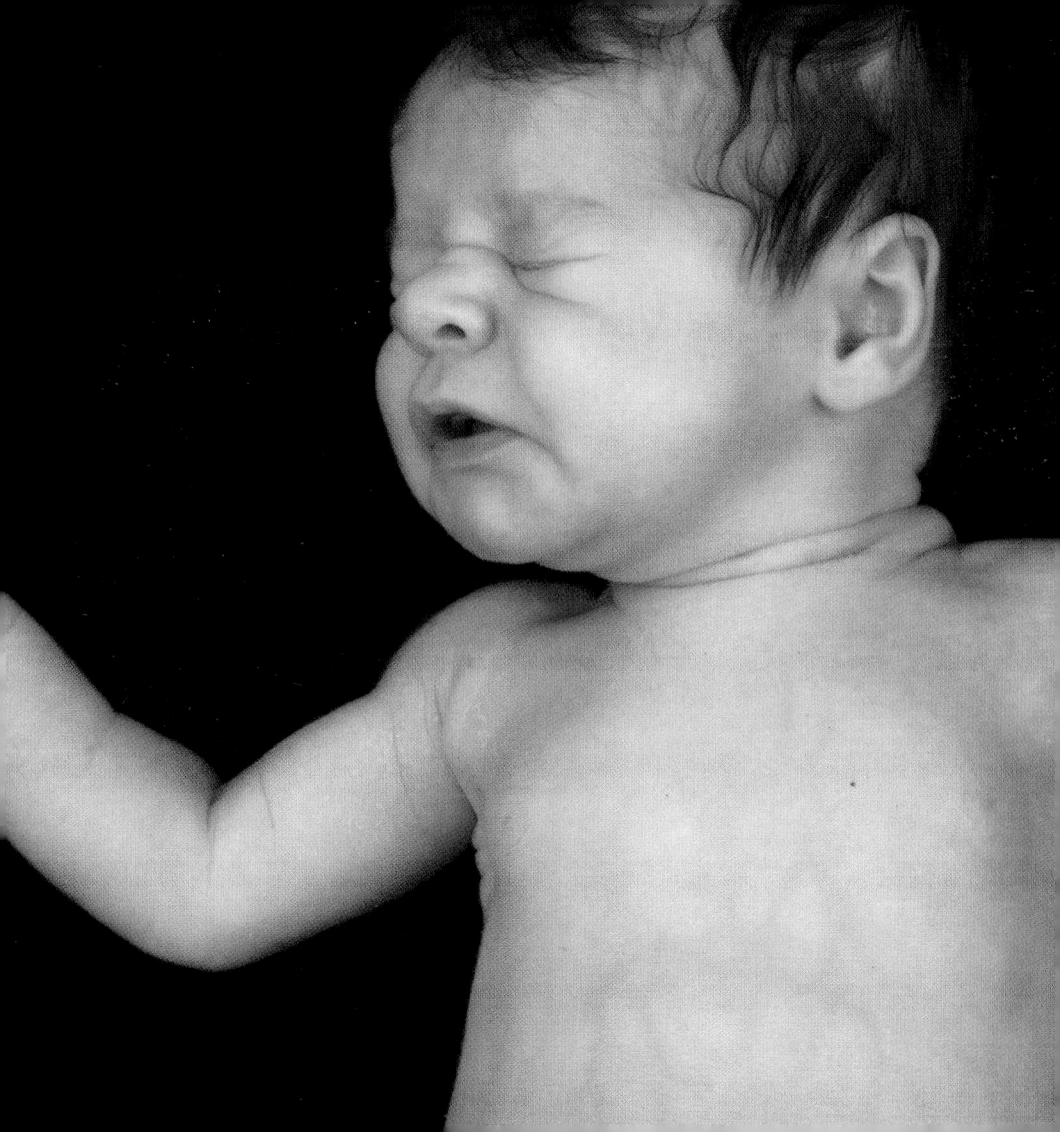

“We never know the love of our parents for us until we have become parents.”

- HENRY WARD BEECHER

"*The quickest way for a parent*

to get a child's attention

is to sit down and look comfortable

- LANE OLINGHOUSE"

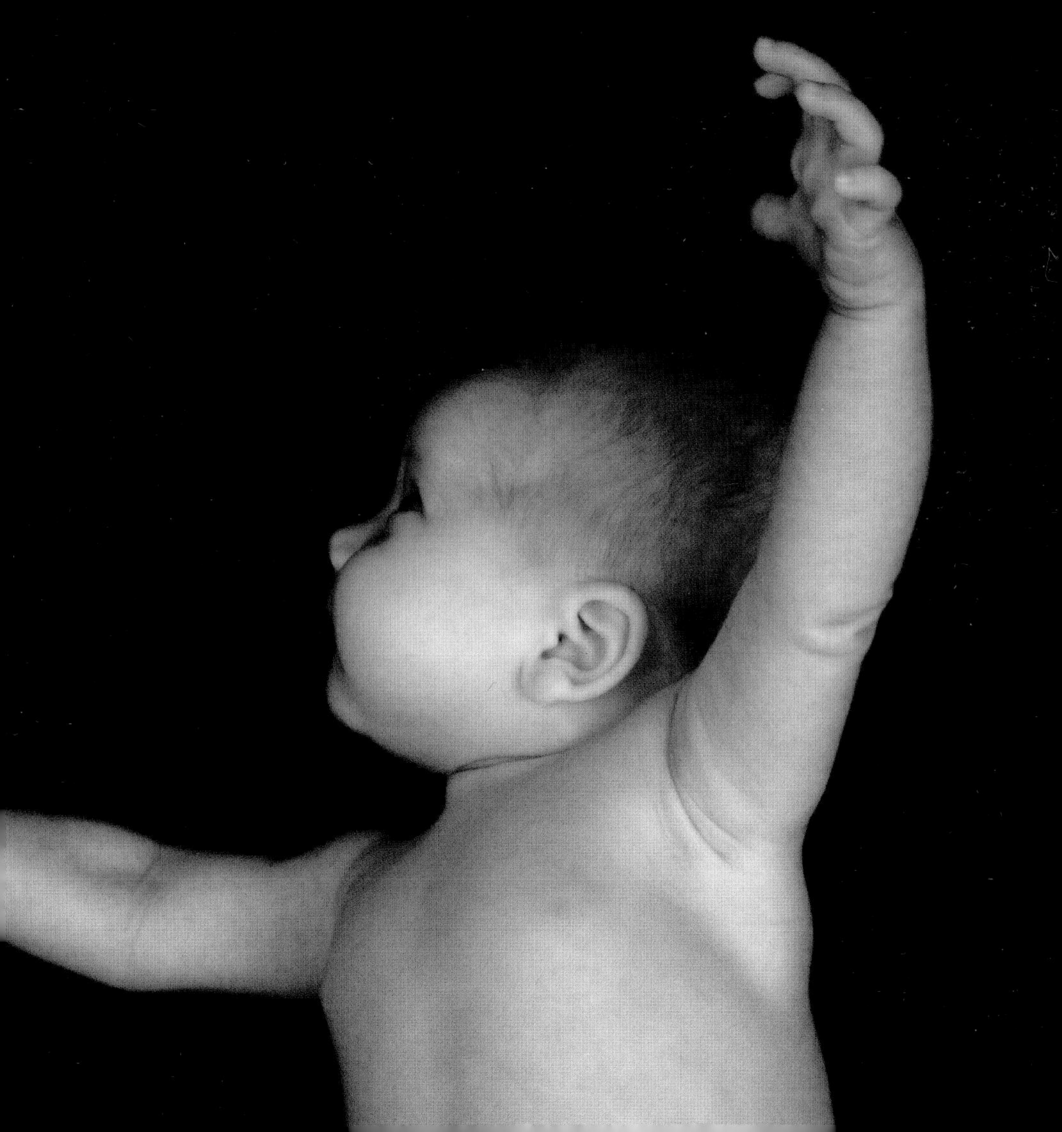

and every mother has it.

- CHINESE PROVERB

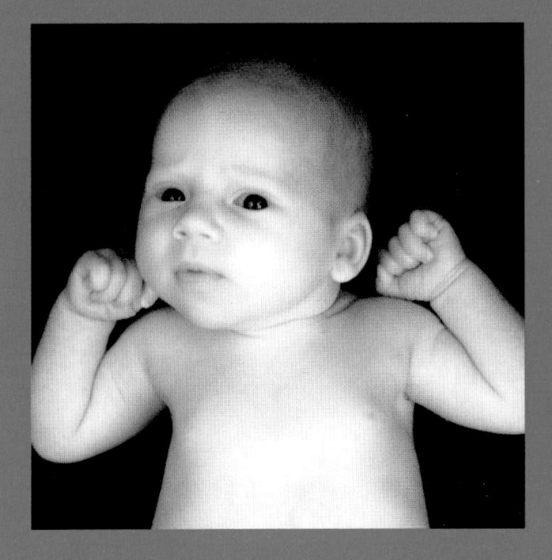

In bringing up children,

spend on them

half as much money

and twice as much time.

- UNKNOWN

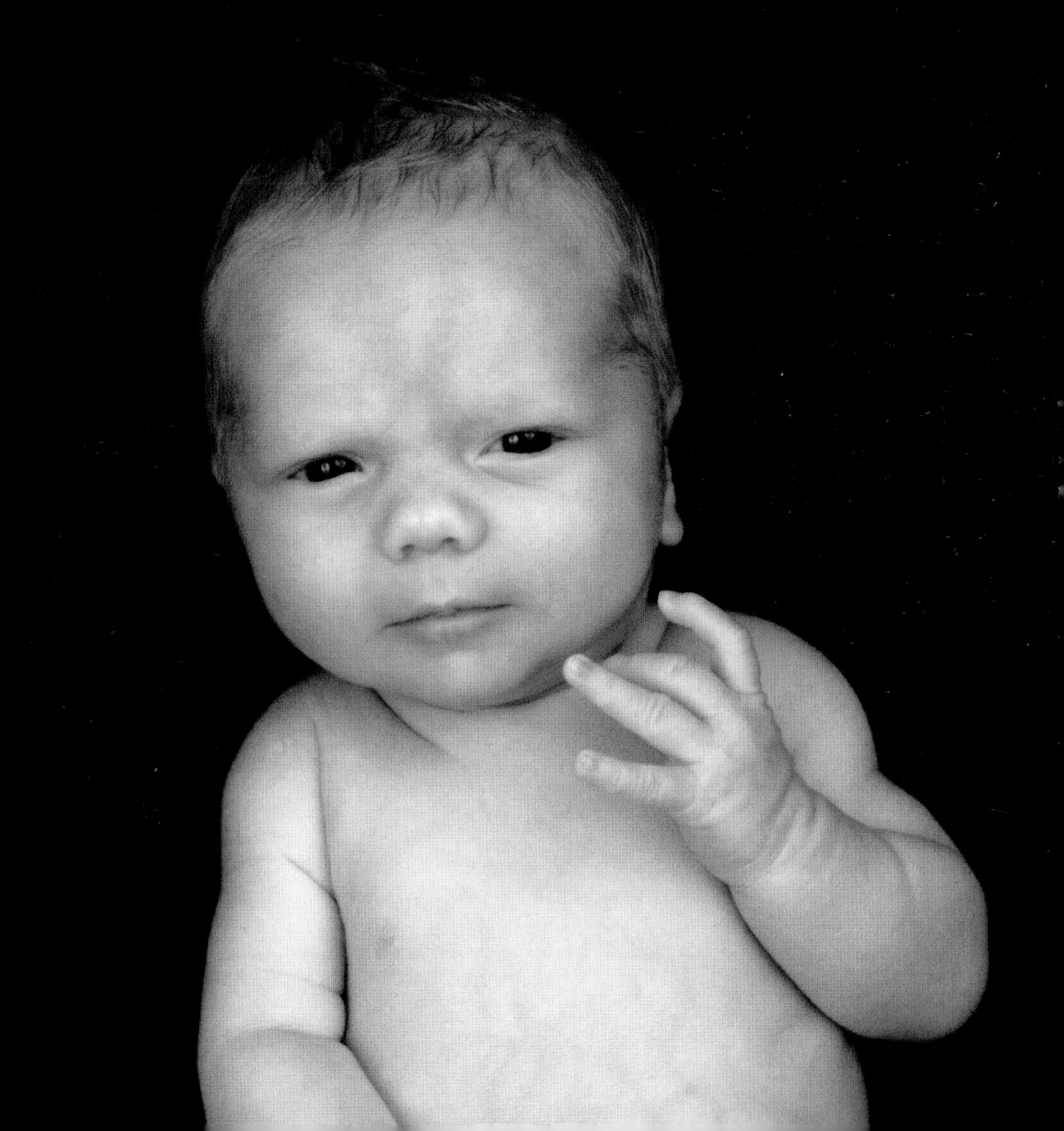

“Babies are always more trouble than you thought

- and more wonderful.”

- **CHARLES OSGOOD**

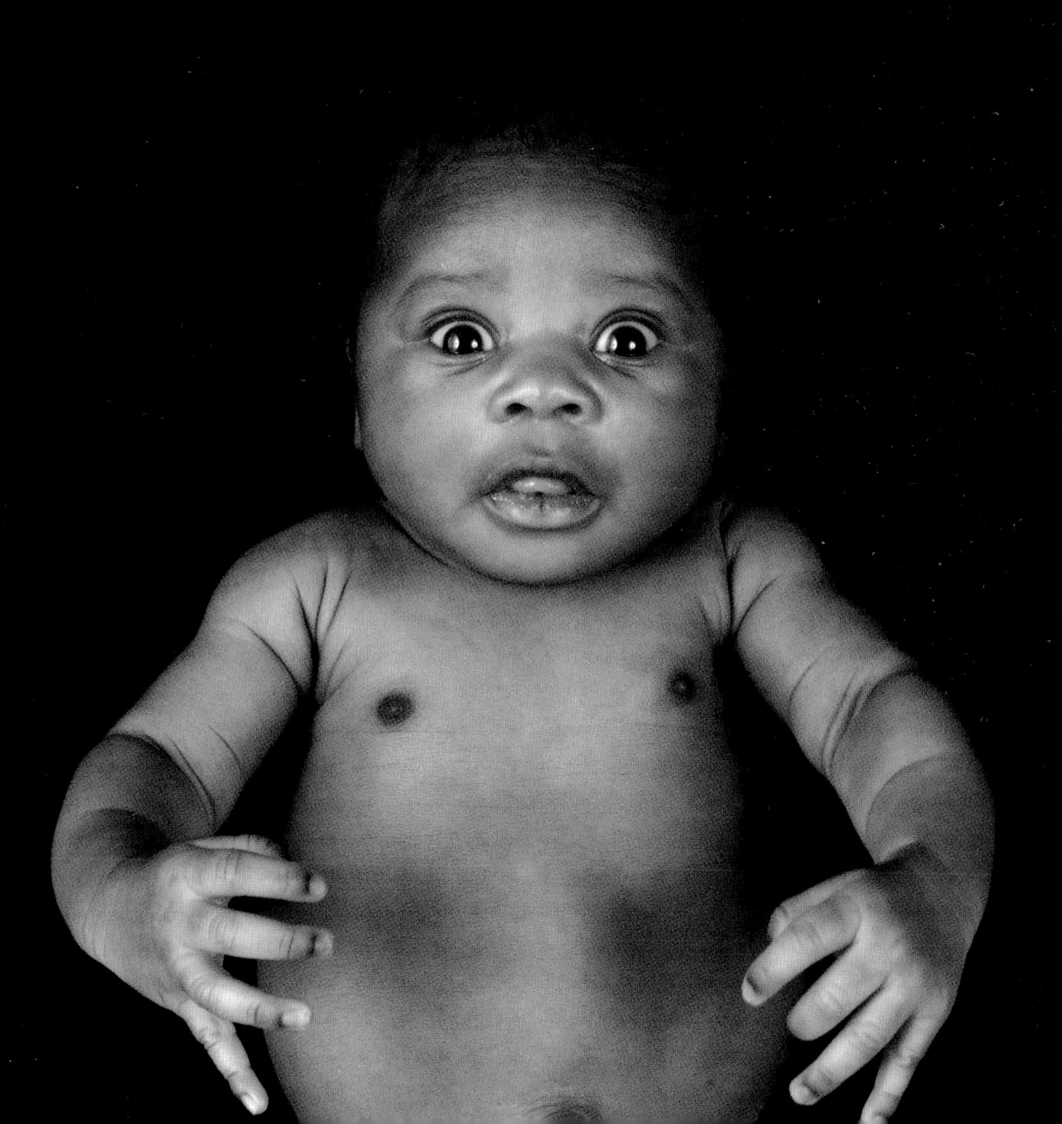

“*Babies* *are such a nice way to start people.*”

- **DON HERROLD**

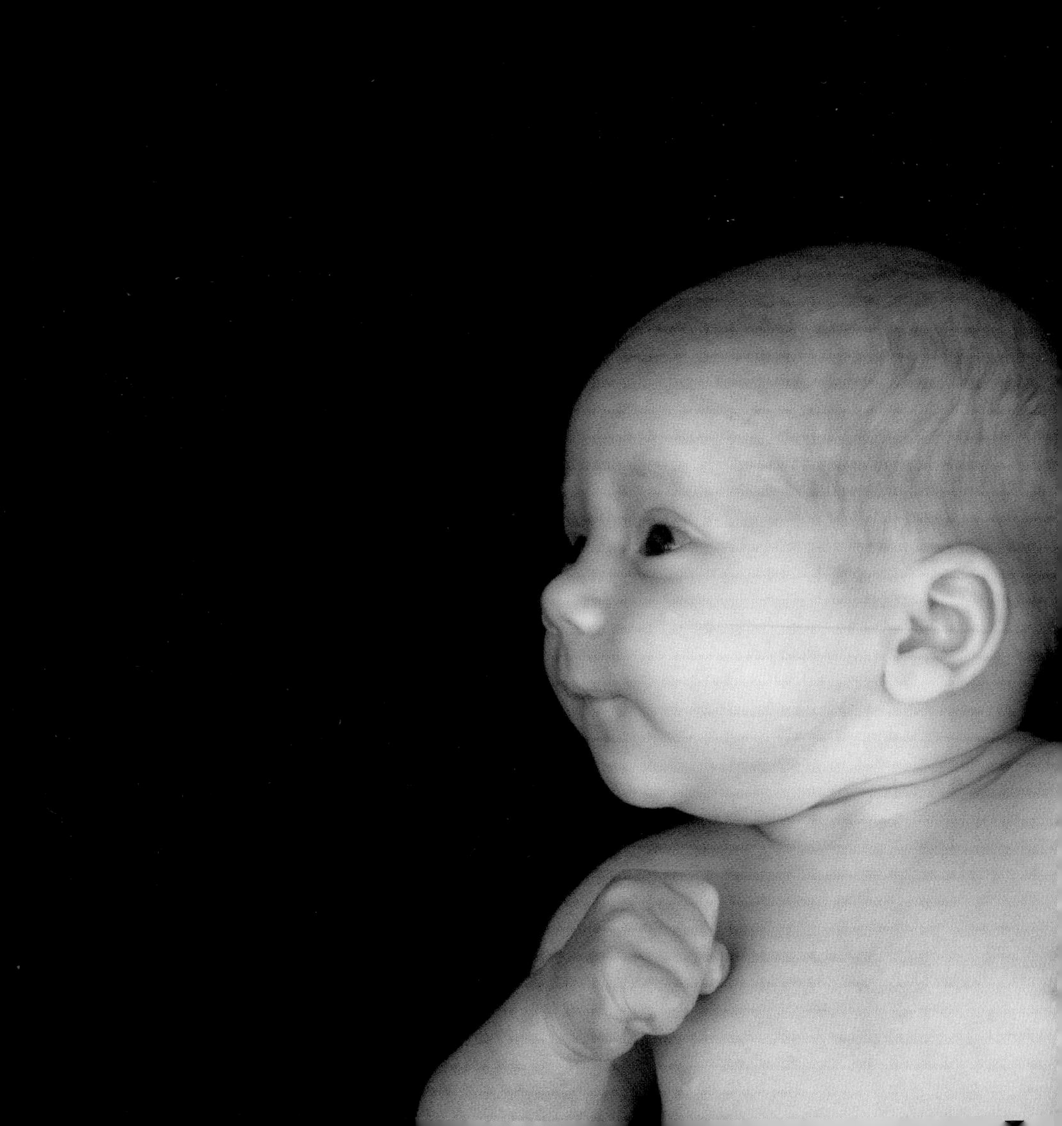

“

I DON'T DISLIKE BABIES,

though I think very young ones rather disgusting.

”

- QUEEN VICTORIA

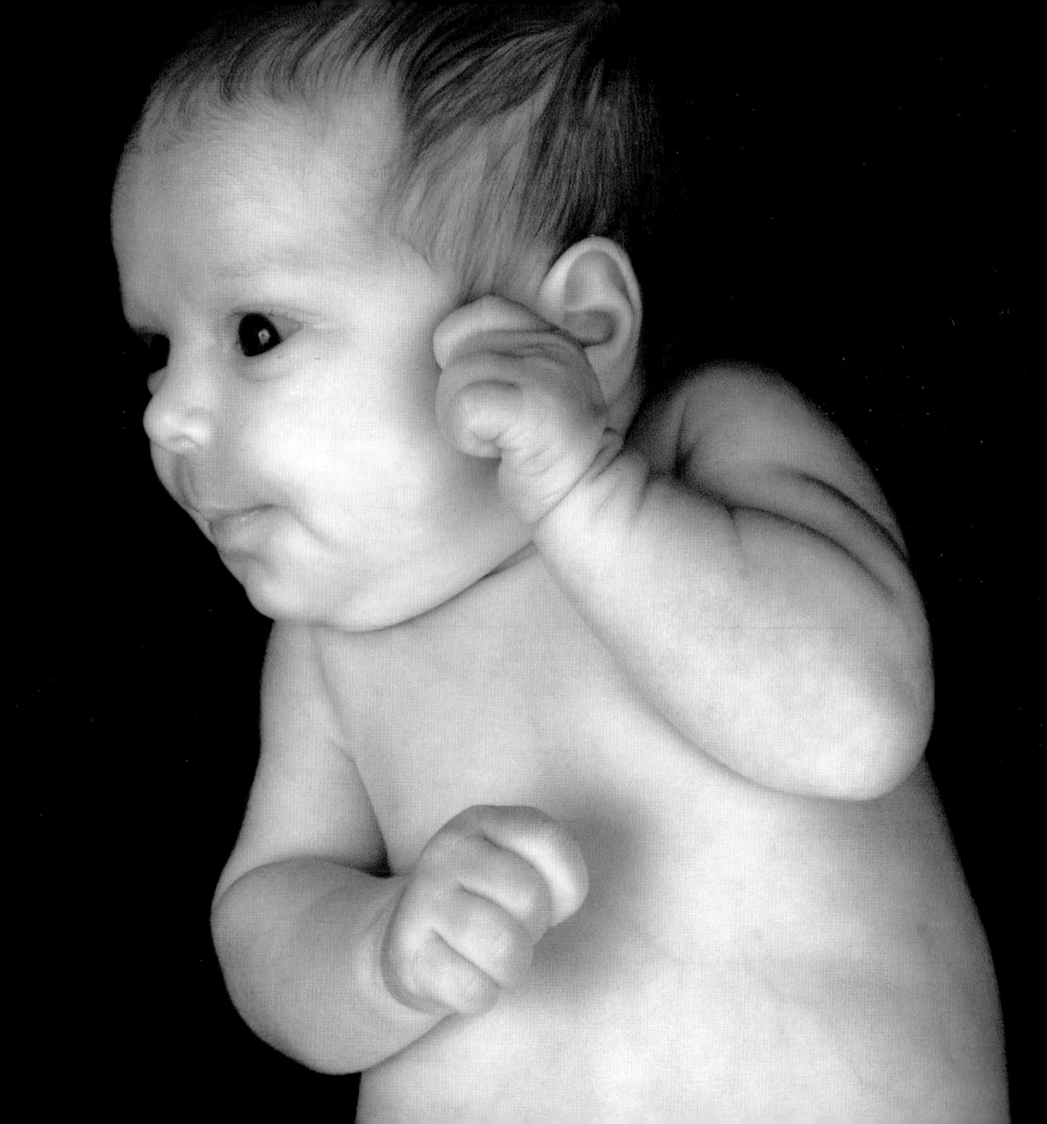

“*The best medicine*

in the world

is a mother's kiss.

- **ANONYMOUS** ”

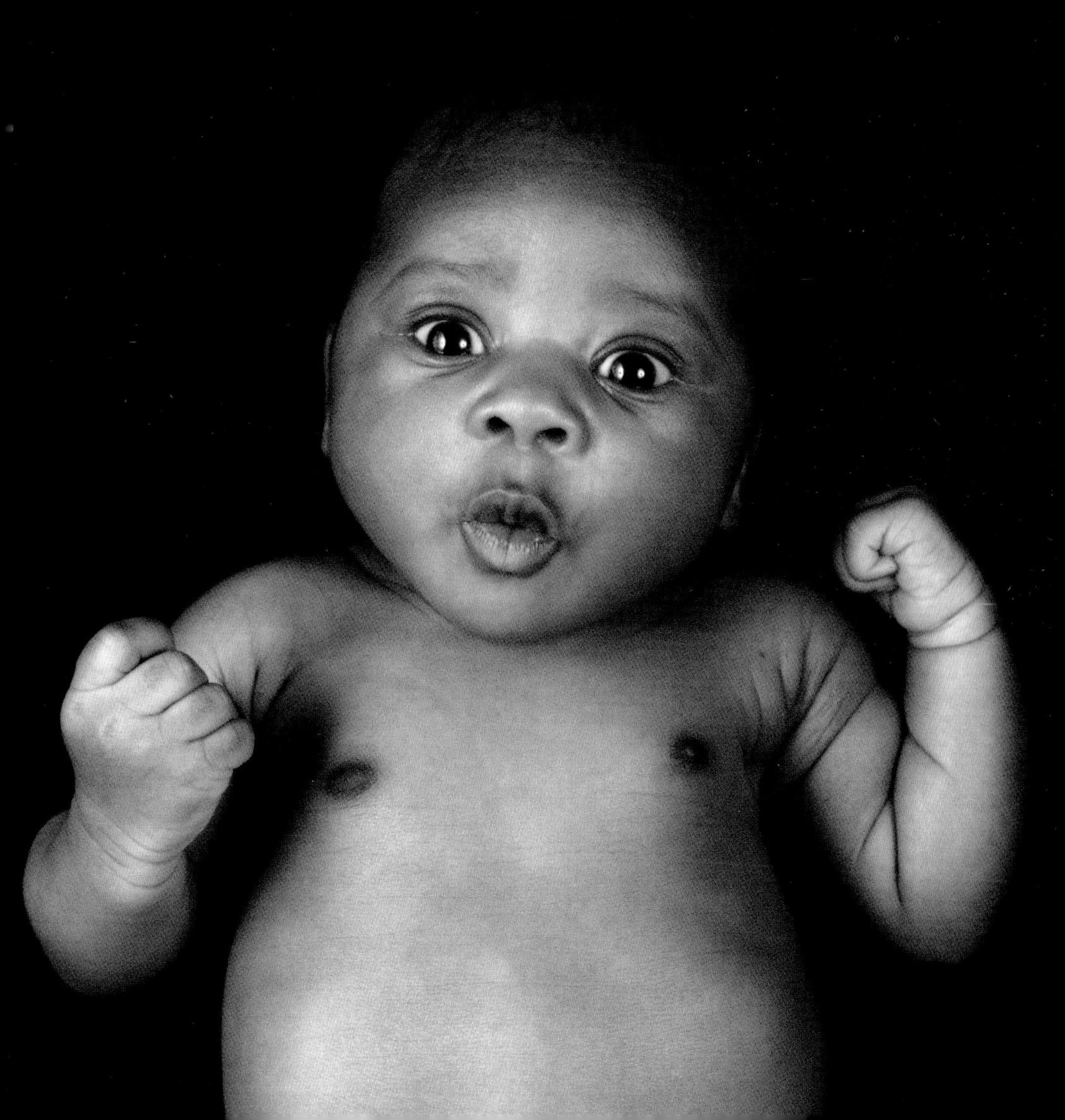

"You couldn't fool you mother
on the foolingest day of your life
even if you had an electrified
fooling machine."

- HOMER SIMPSON

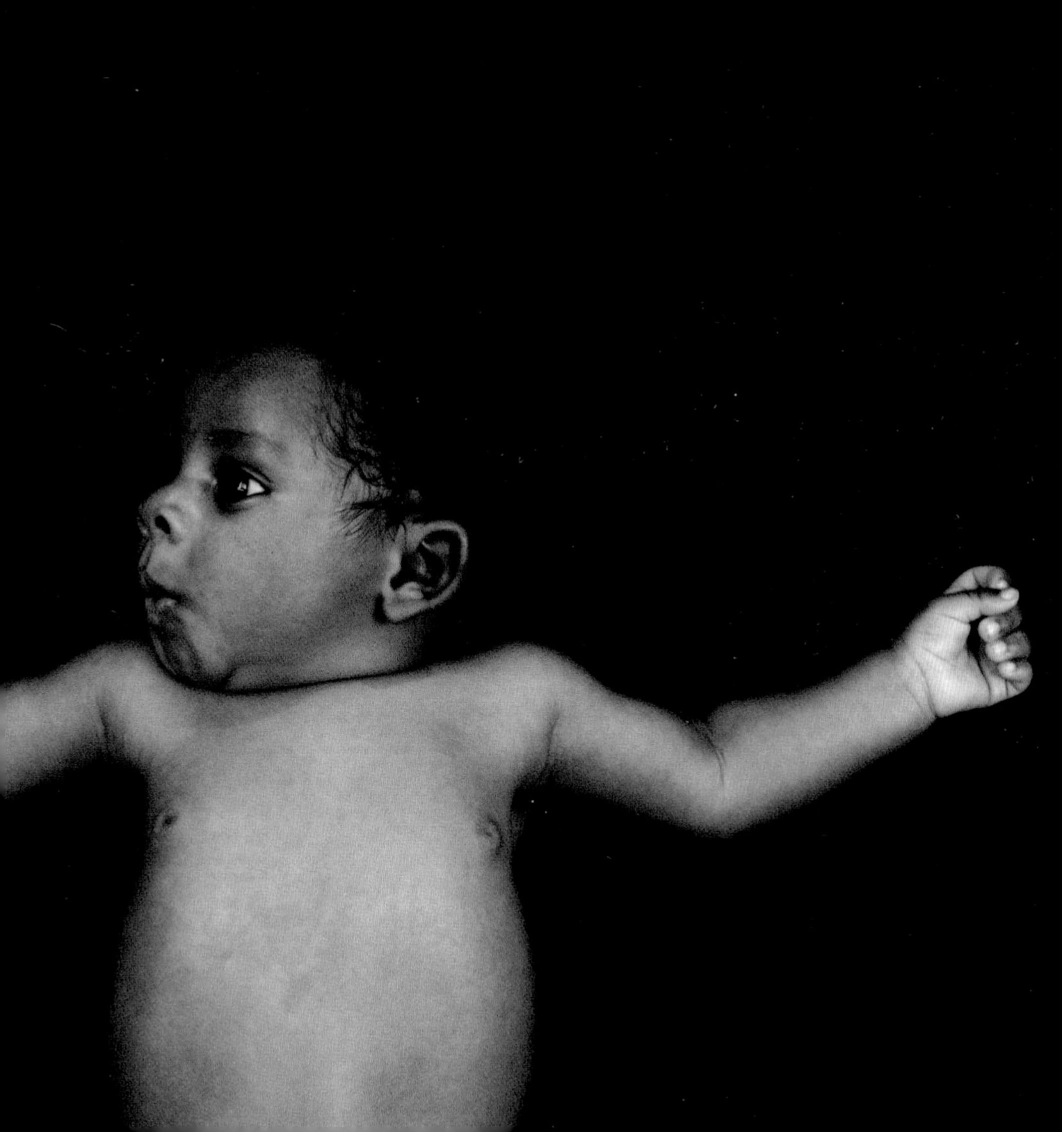

“*The hand that rocks the cradle*
is the hand that rules the world.”

- W.R. WALLACE

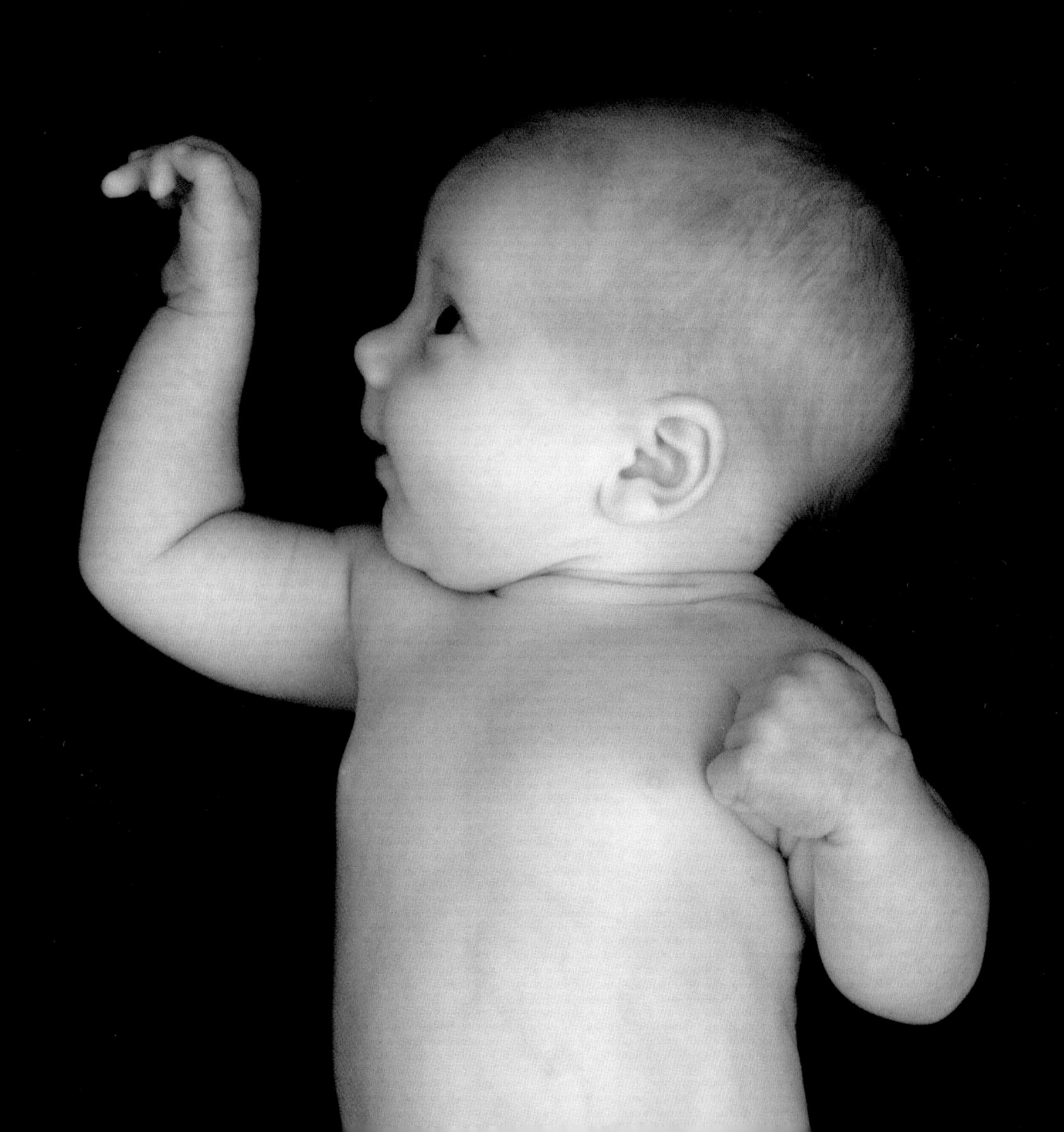

"

100's

A good mother is worth hundreds of schoolmasters.

- GEORGE HERBERT

"

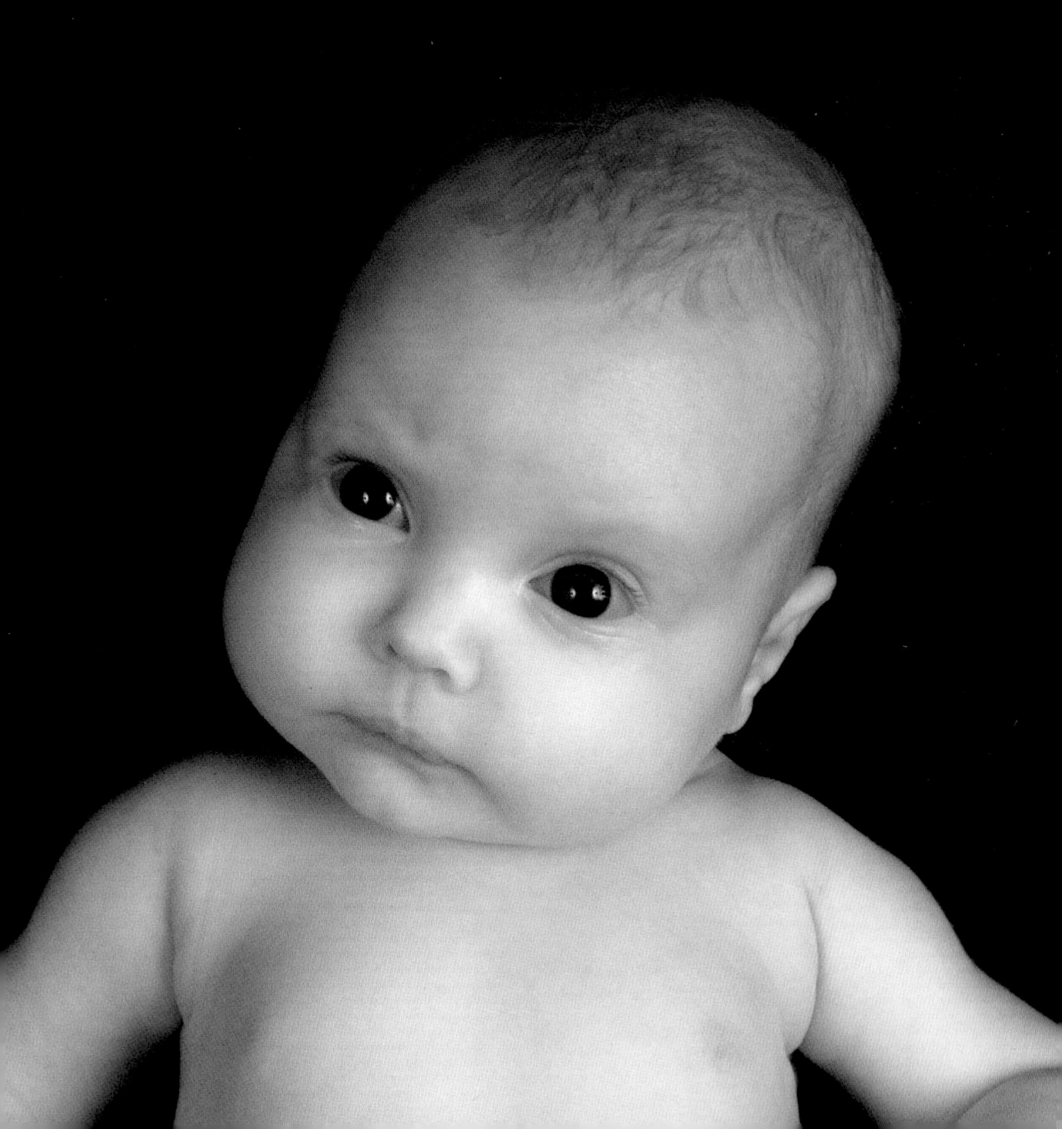

“Children
are the
true
connoisseurs.

What's
precious
to them
has no price,
only value.”

- BEL KAUFMAN

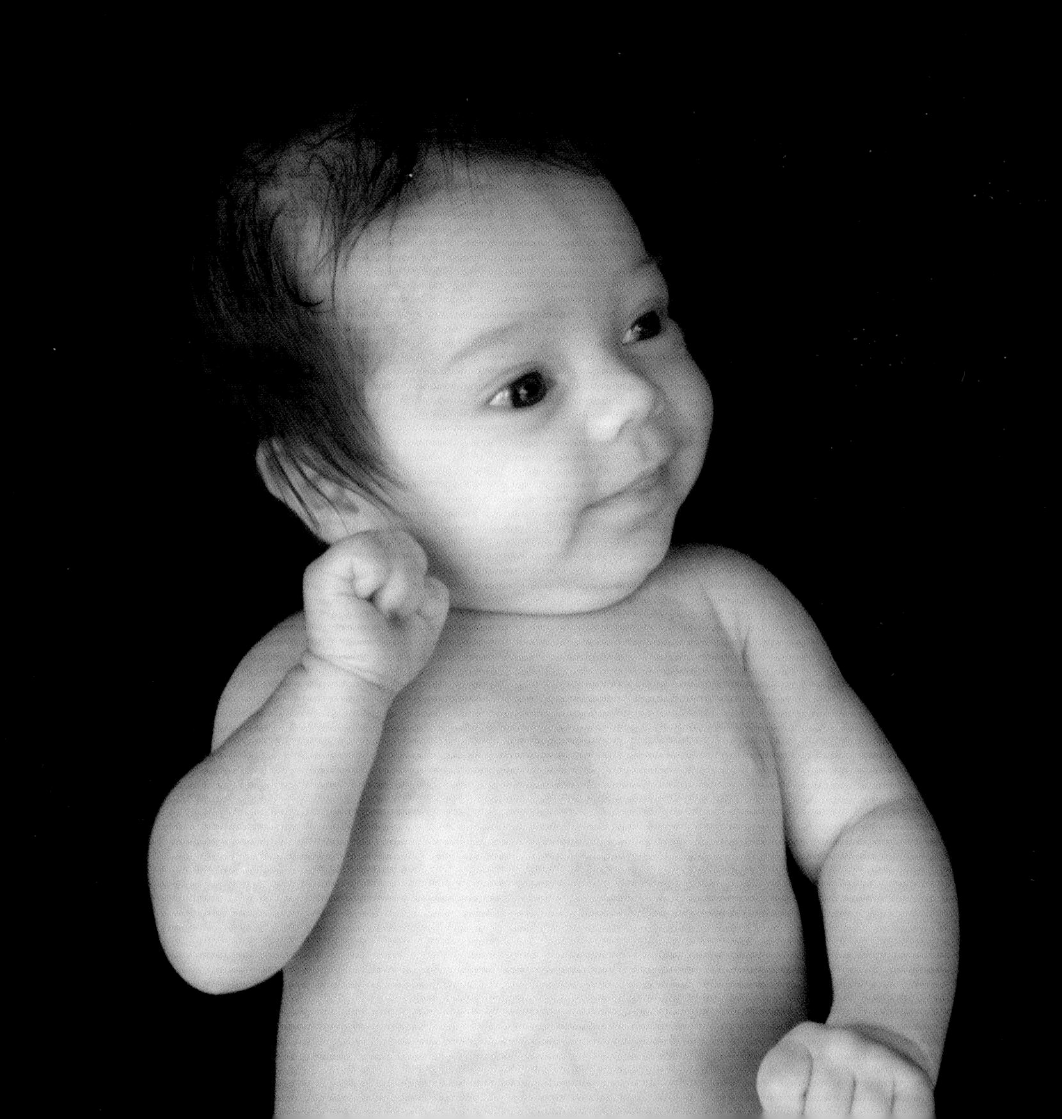

“

When you are a mother,

you are never really alone in your thoughts.

A mother always has to think twice,

once for herself and once for her child.

”

- SOPHIA LOREN

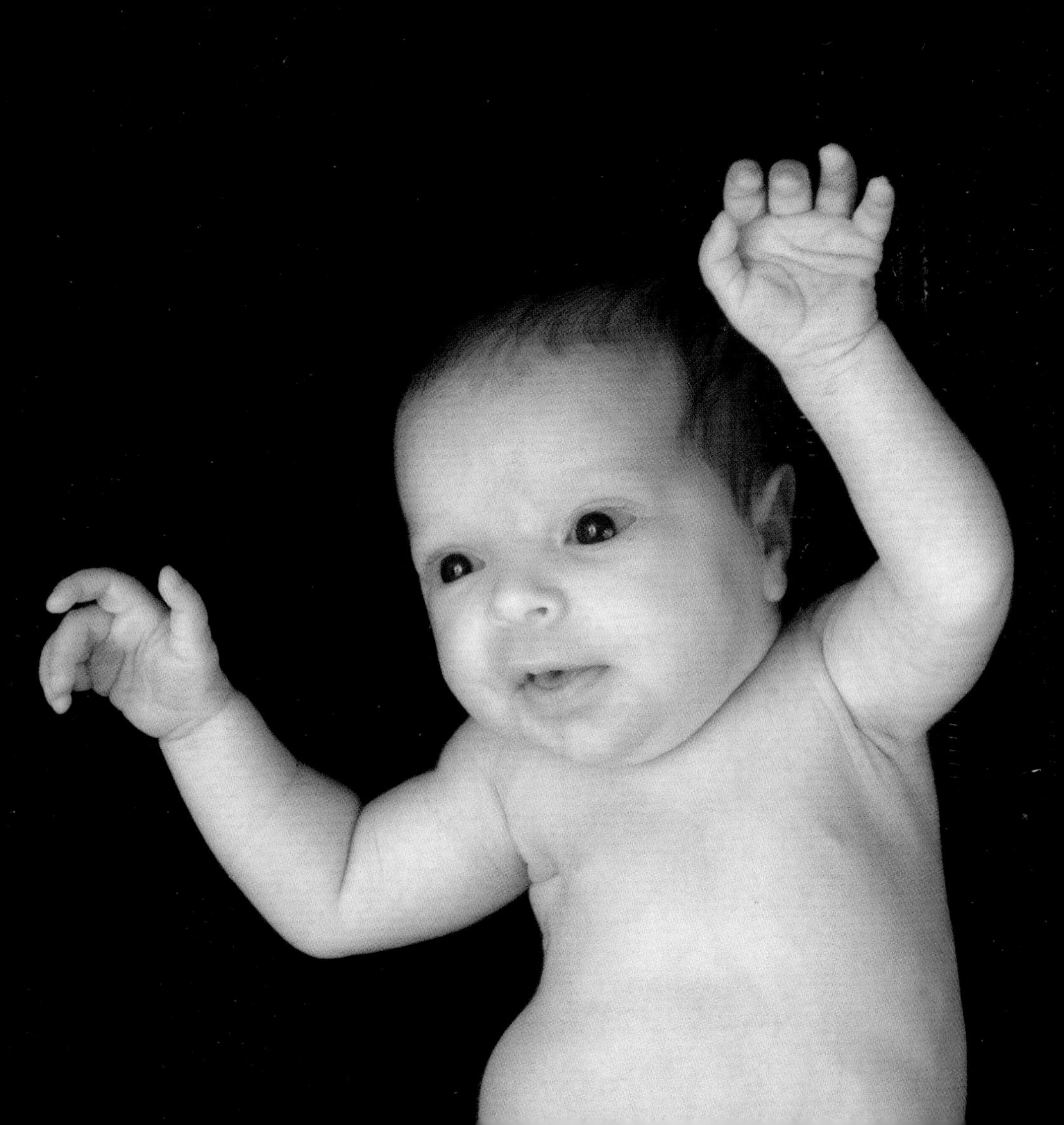

"A mother's arms are made of tenderness and children sleep soundly in them."

- VICTOR HUGO

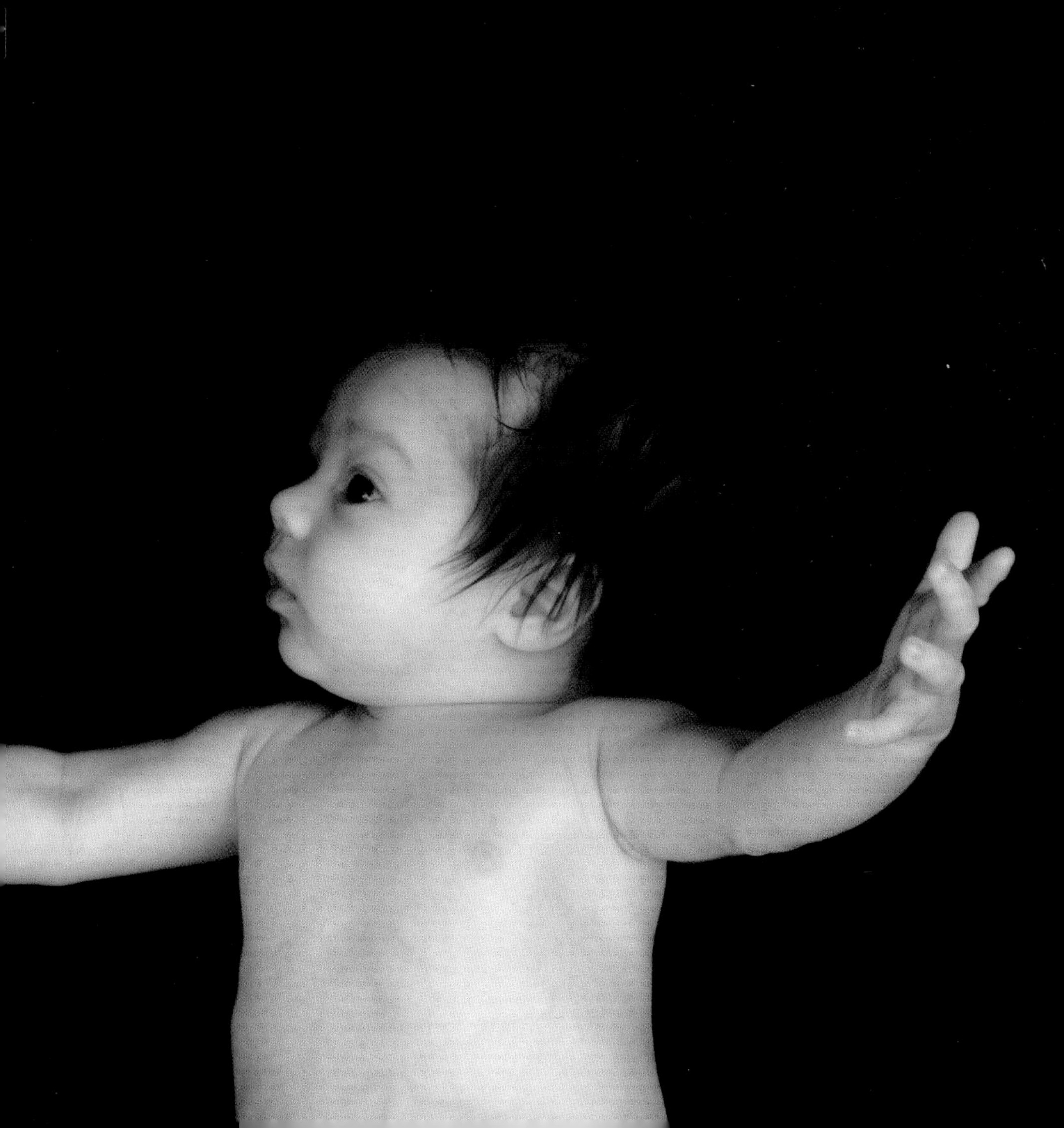

“

It's not easy

being a mother.

If it were easy,

fathers would do it.

”

- THE GOLDEN GIRLS

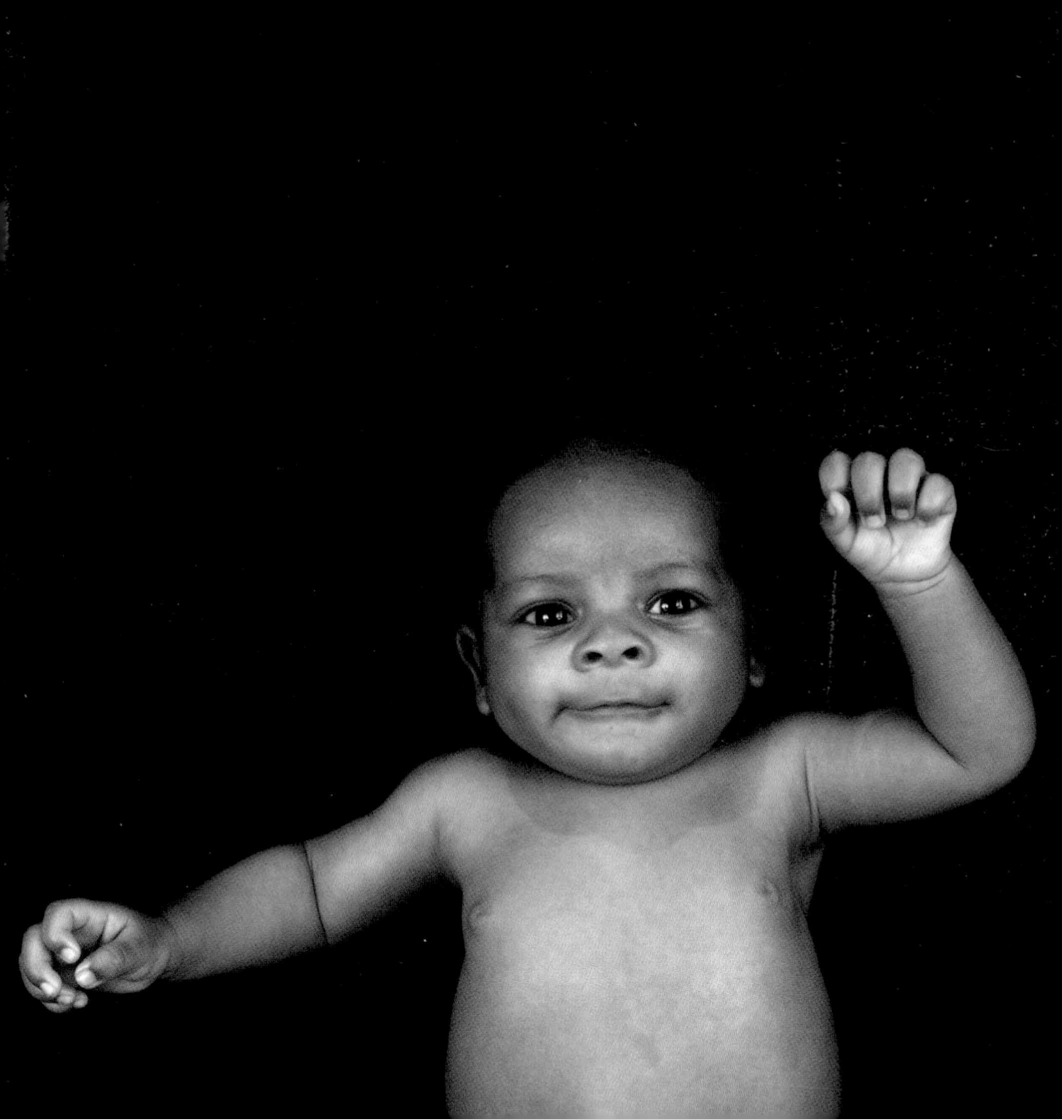

“*A mother is*

she who can take the place of all others

but whose place no one else can take.”

- CARDINAL MERMILLOD

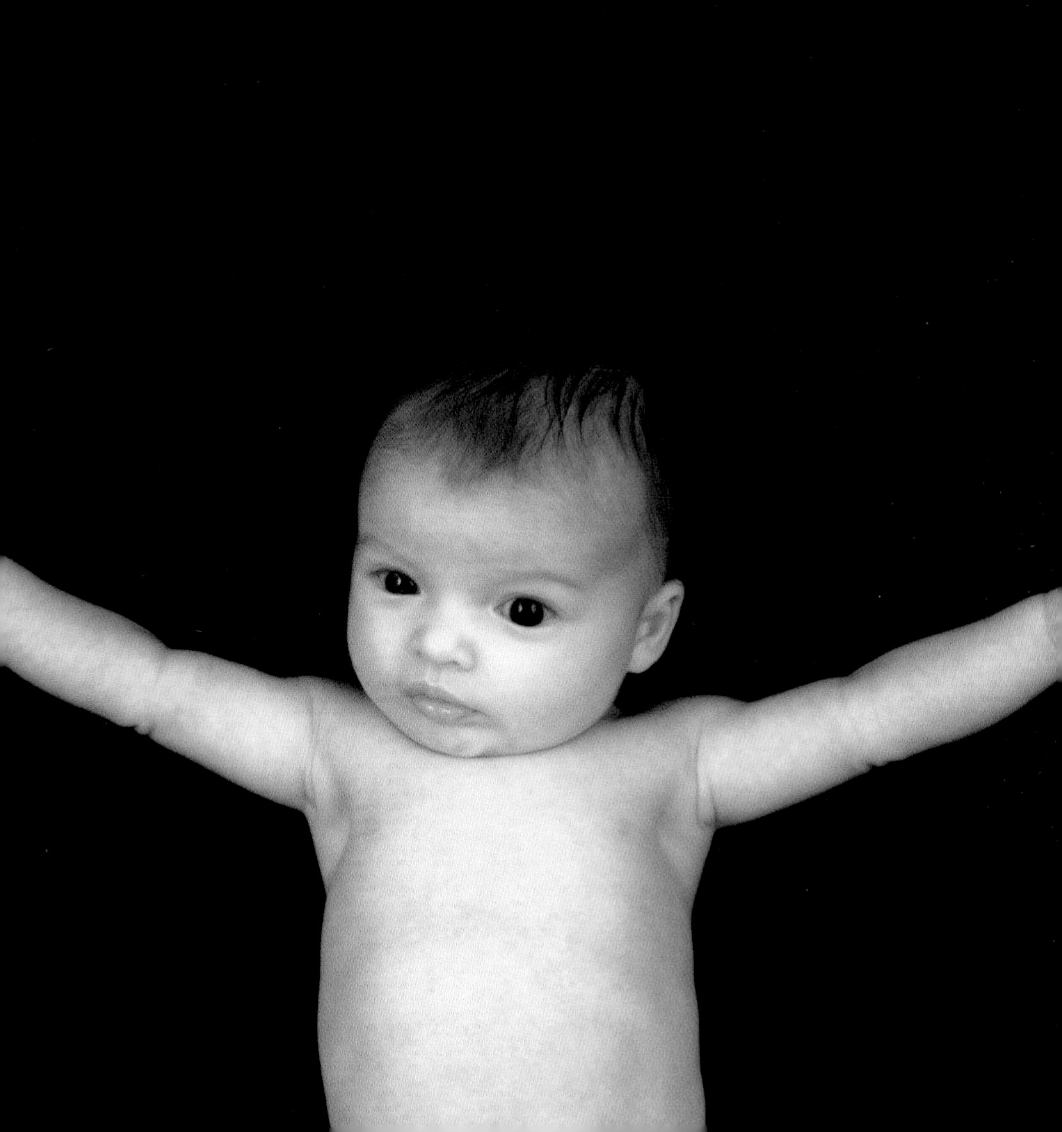

It will be gone before you know it.

The fingerprints on the wall

appear higher and higher.

Then suddenly they disappear.

”

- **DOROTHY EVSLIN**

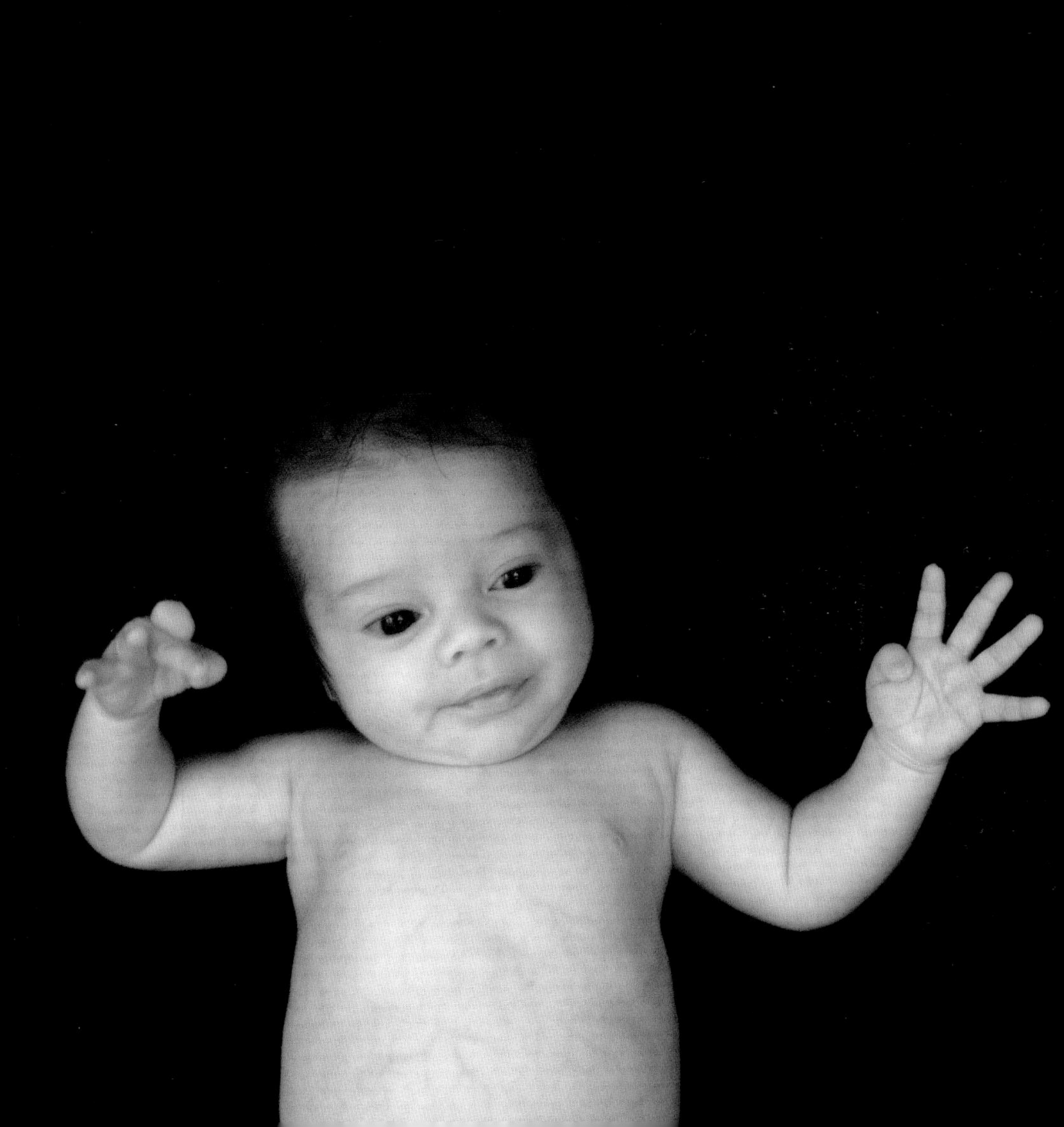

“A

A woman with a child rediscovers the world. All is changed - politics, loyalties, needs. For now all is judged by the life of the child...and of all the children.

”

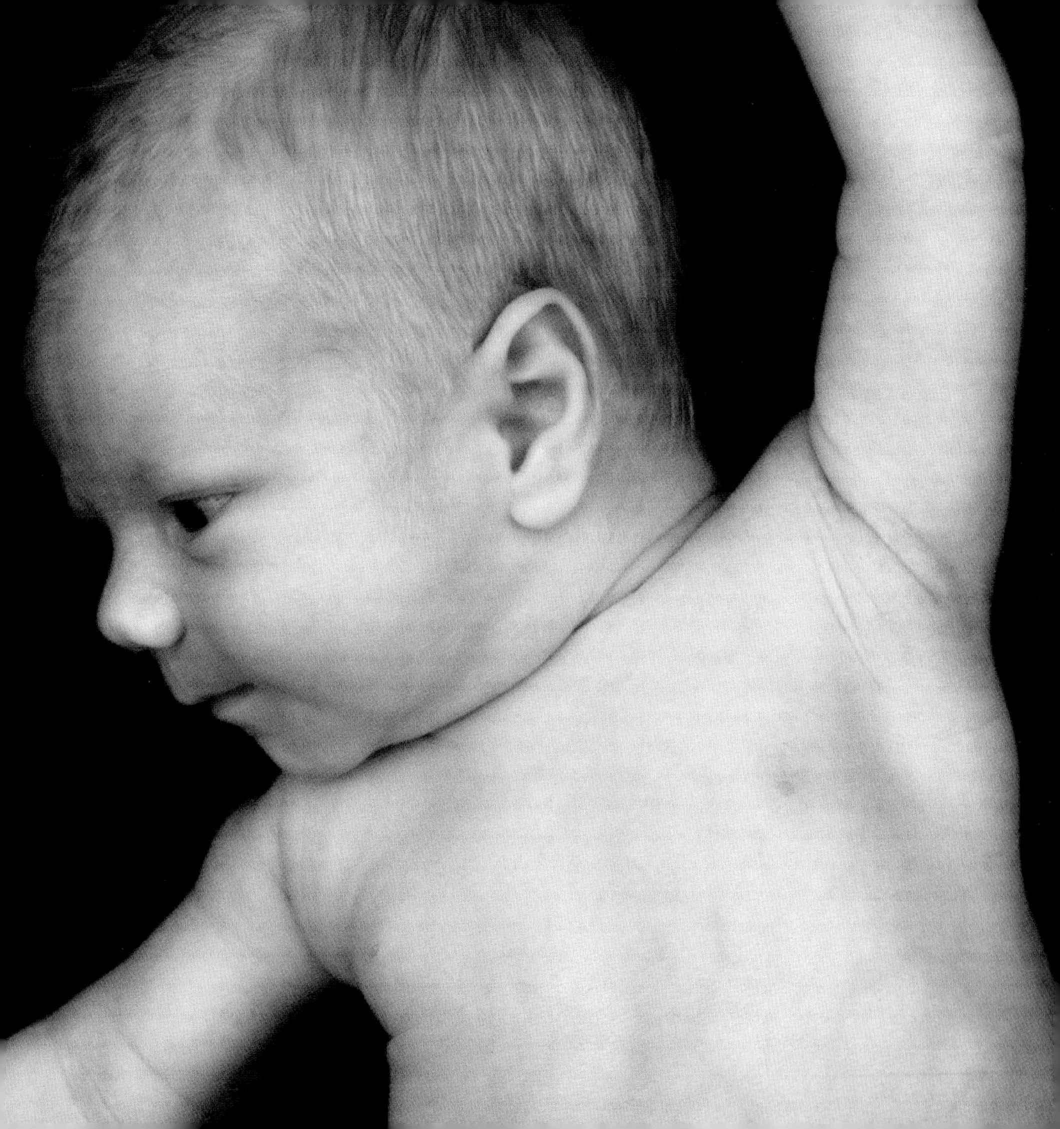

“

The most effective form of birth control I know is spending the day with my kids.

”

- JILL BENSLEY

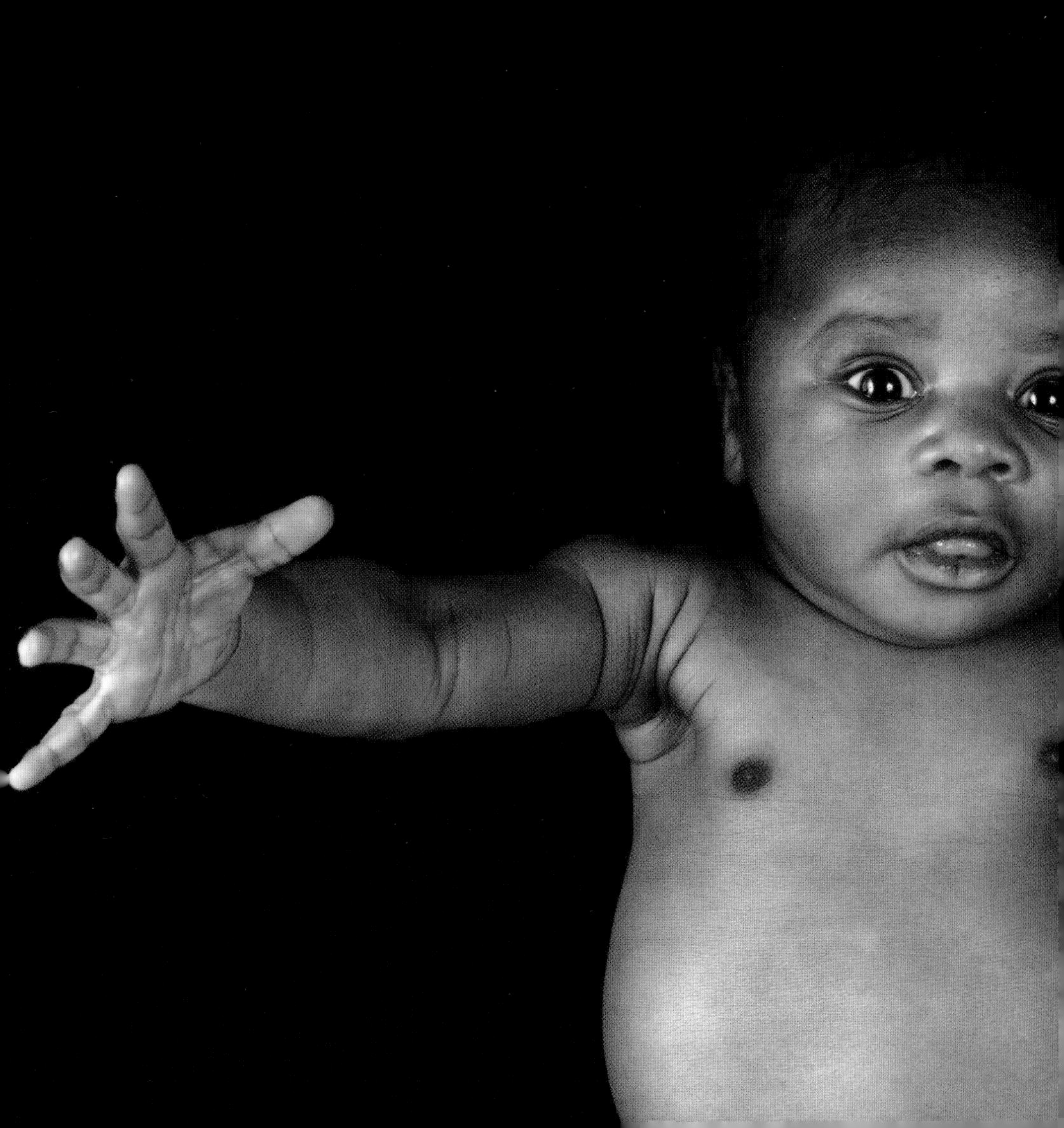

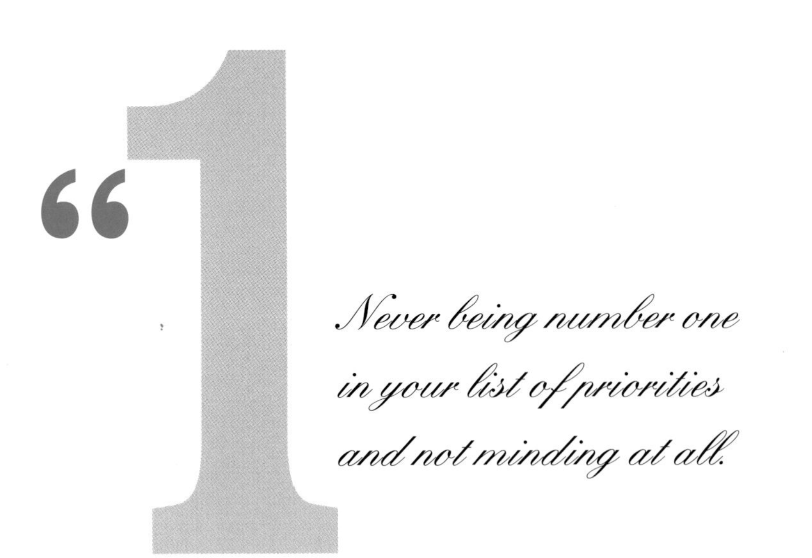

"Never being number one in your list of priorities and not minding at all."

- JASMINE GUINNESS

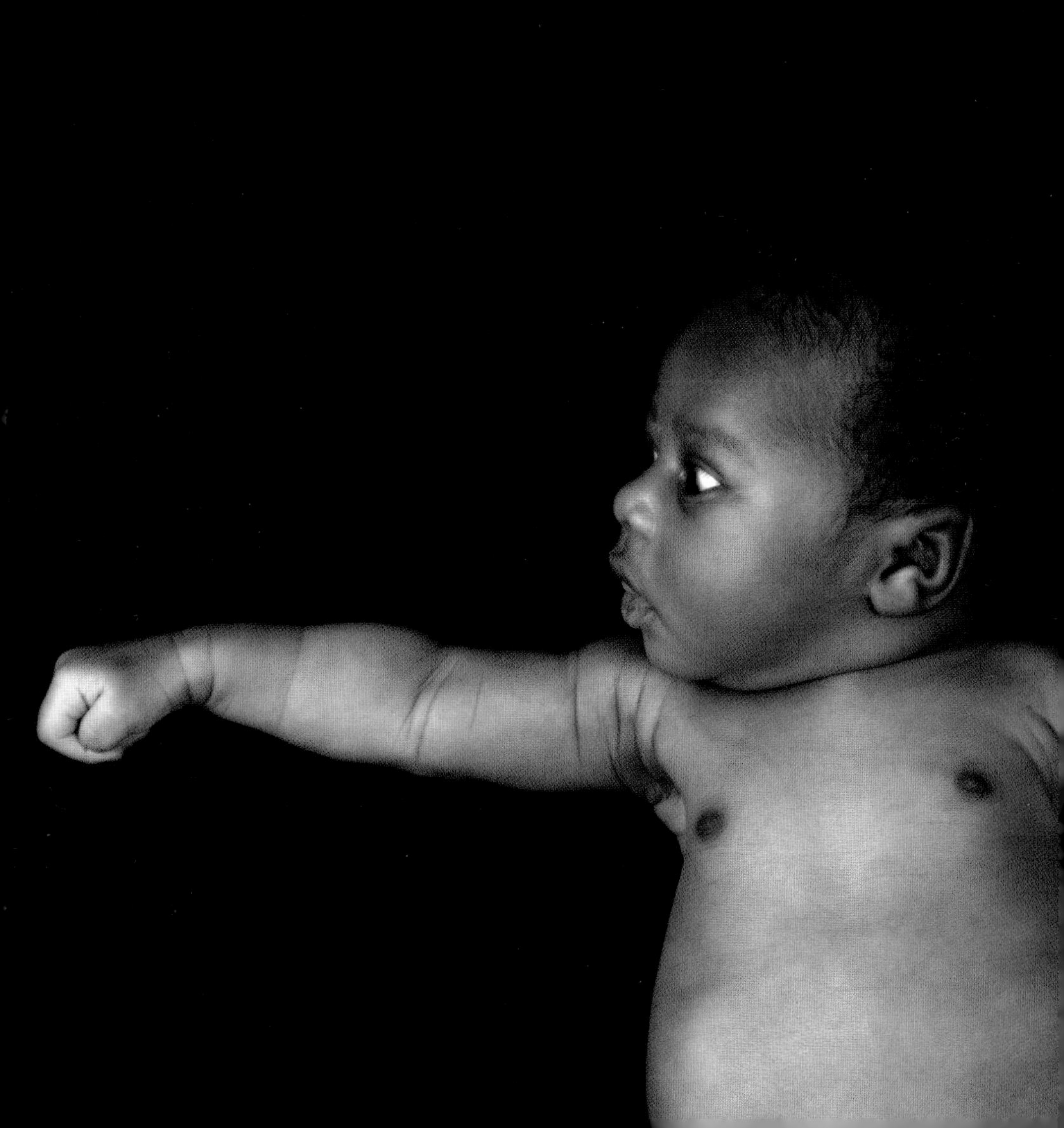

“*The best thing*

you can give children,

next to good habits,

are good memories.”

- **SYDNEY J HARRIS**

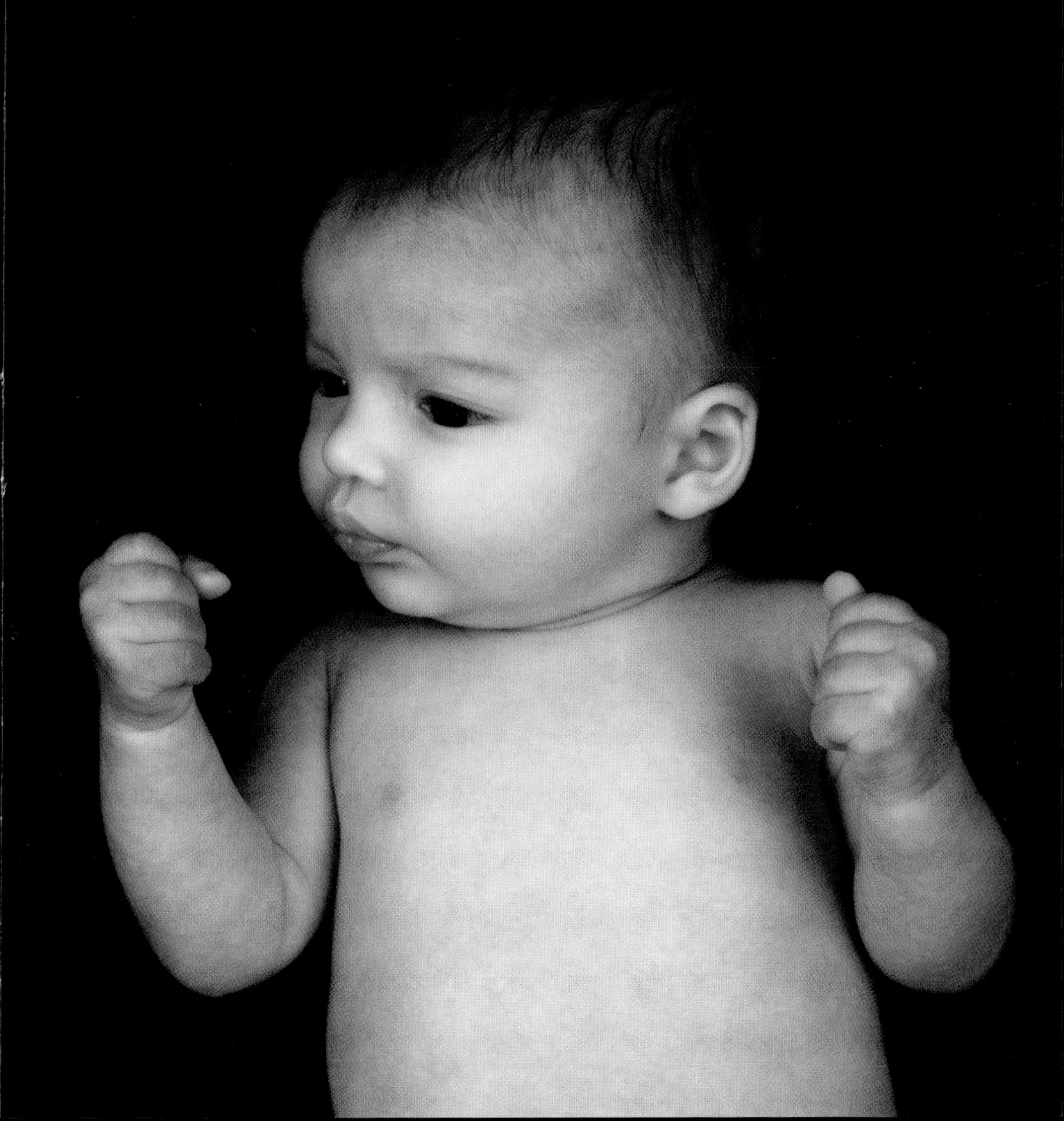

“*There never was a child so lovely*
but his mother was glad to get him asleep.”

- RALPH WALDO EMERSON

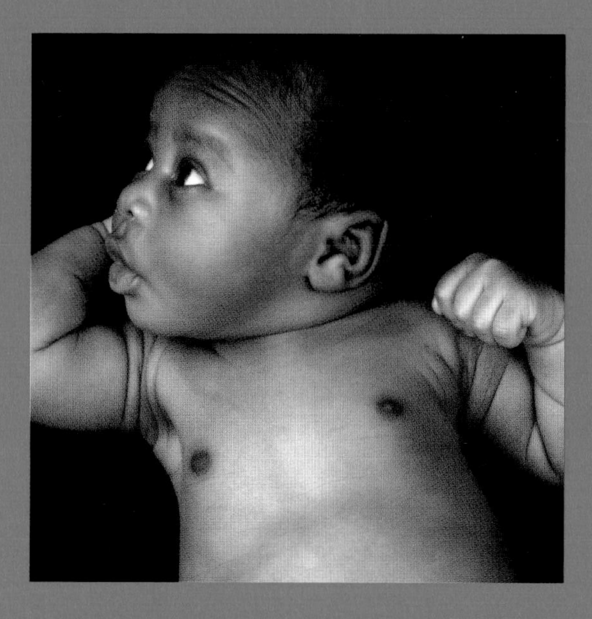

“

The soul is healed by being with children.

”

- **FYODOR DOSTOYEVSKI**

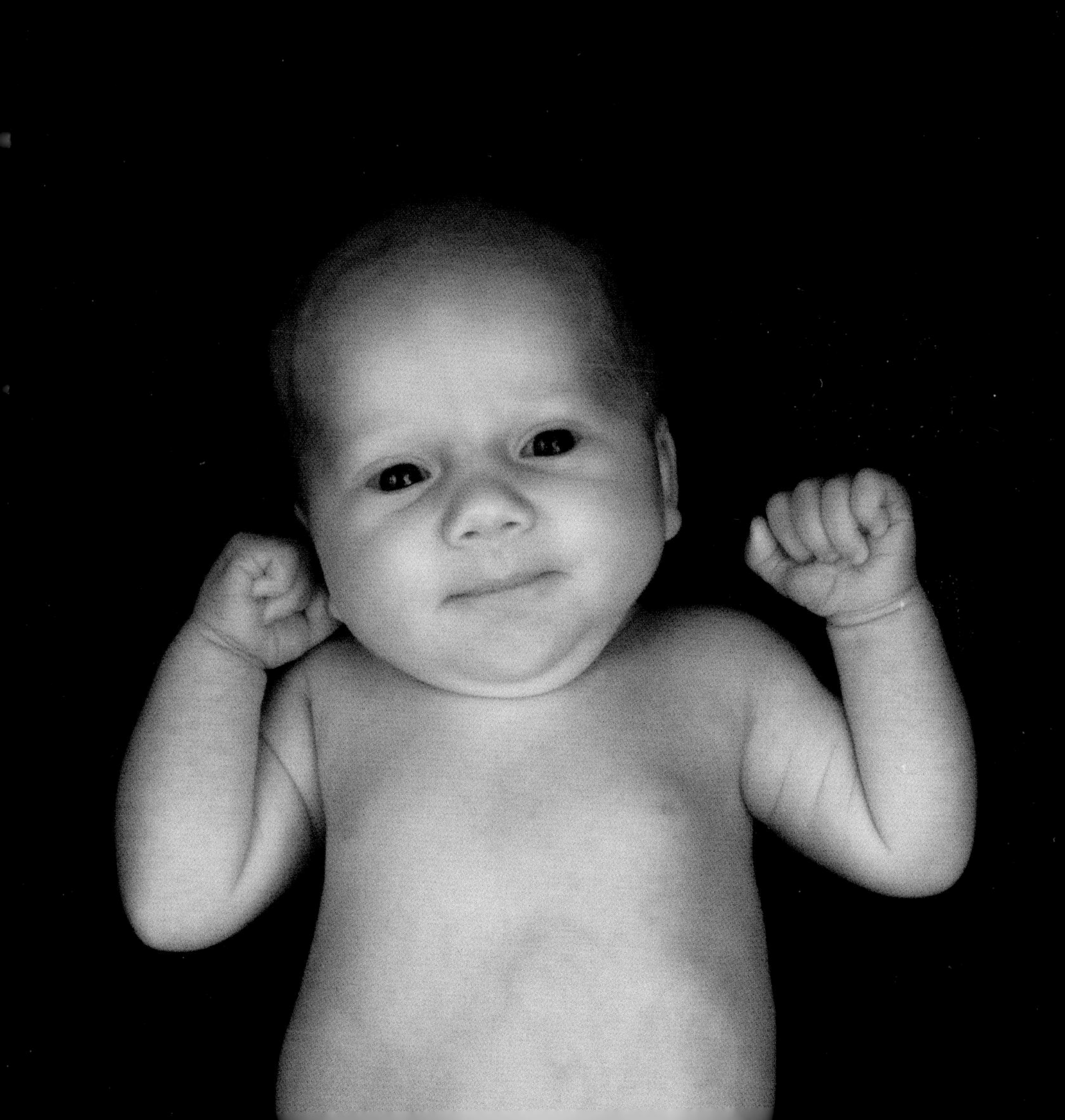

“

PARENTHOOD

remains the greatest single preserve of the amateur.

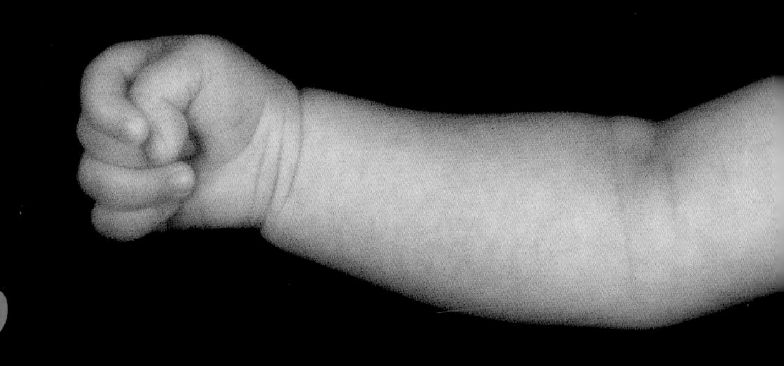

”

- ALVIN TOFFLER

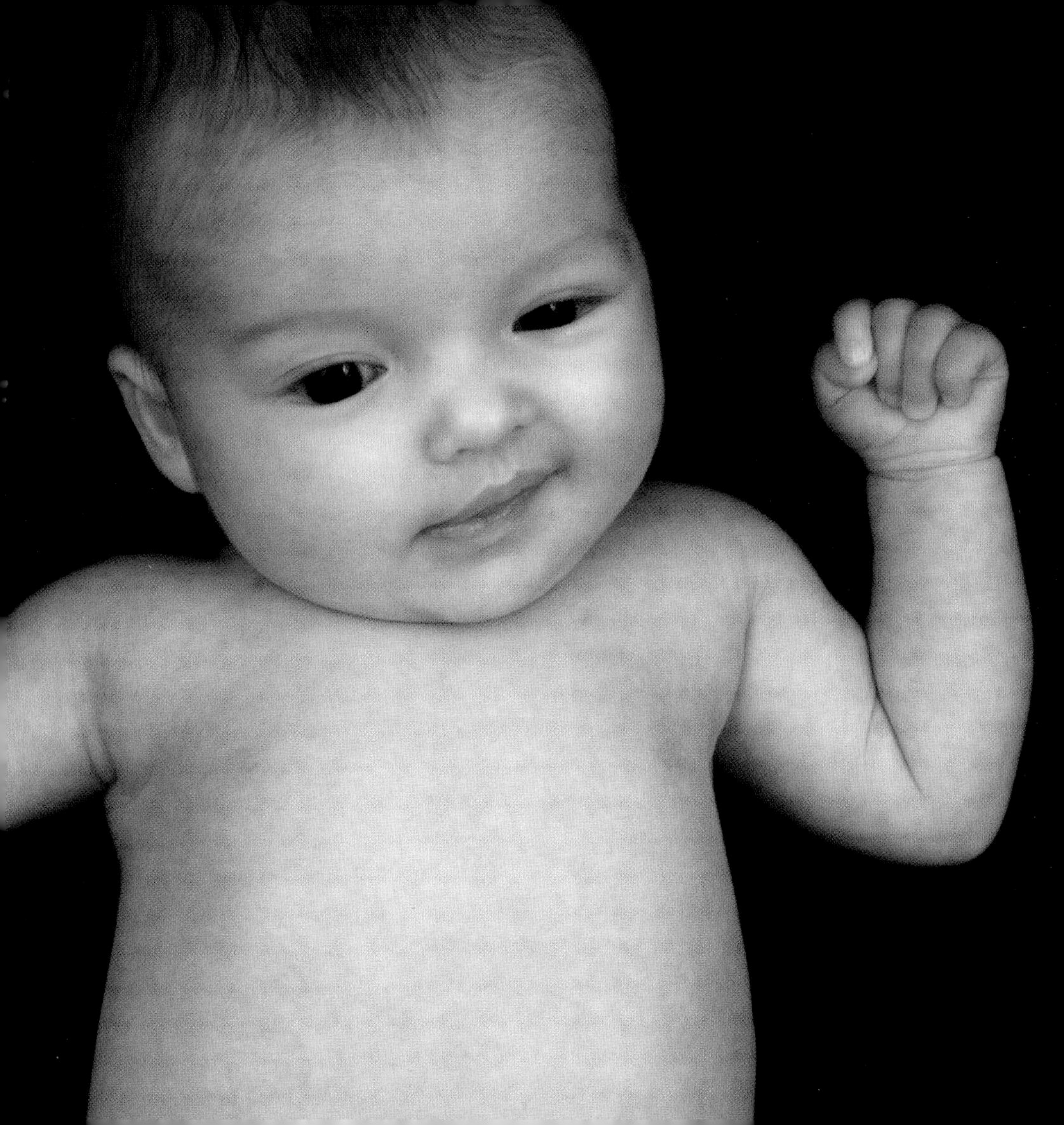

“A baby is born with a need to be loved and never outgrows it.”

- FRANK A CLARK

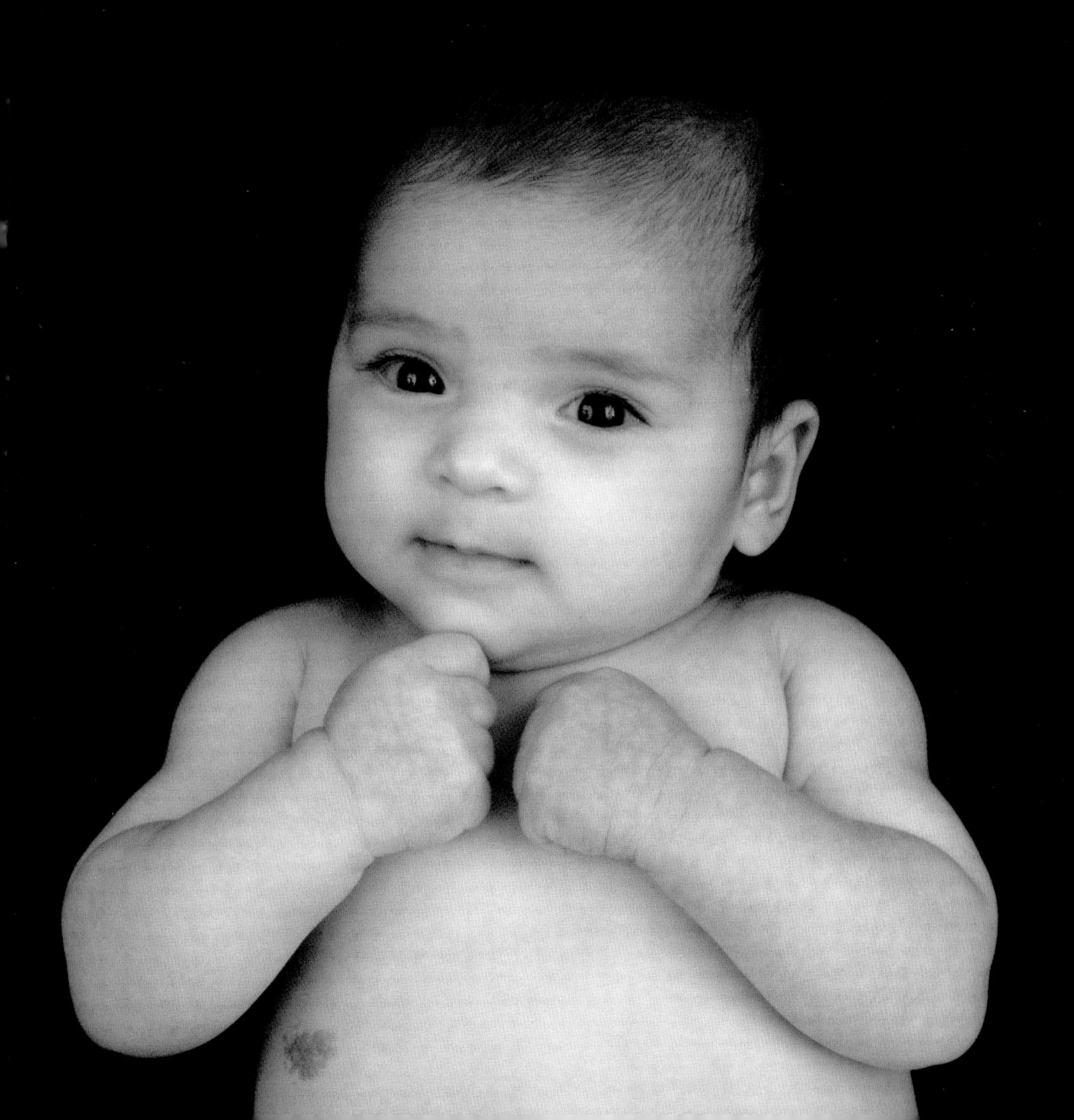

“

The role of ***mother*** *is probably the most important career a woman can have.*

”

- JANET MARY RILEY

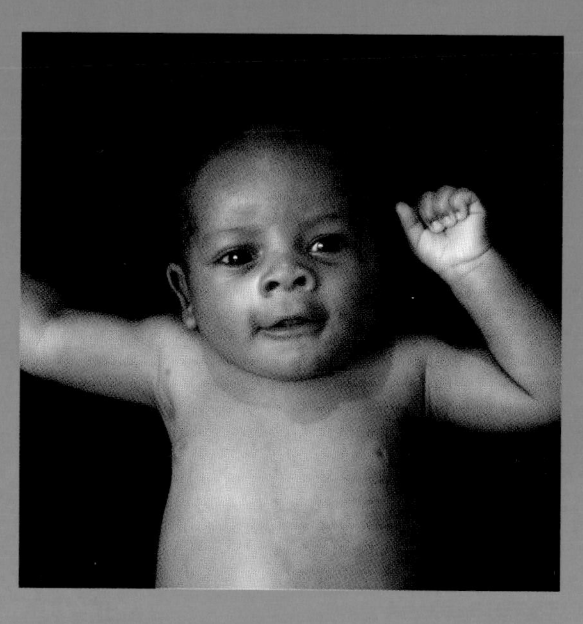

Any mother could perform the jobs

of several air-traffic controllers with ease.

- **LISA ALTHER**

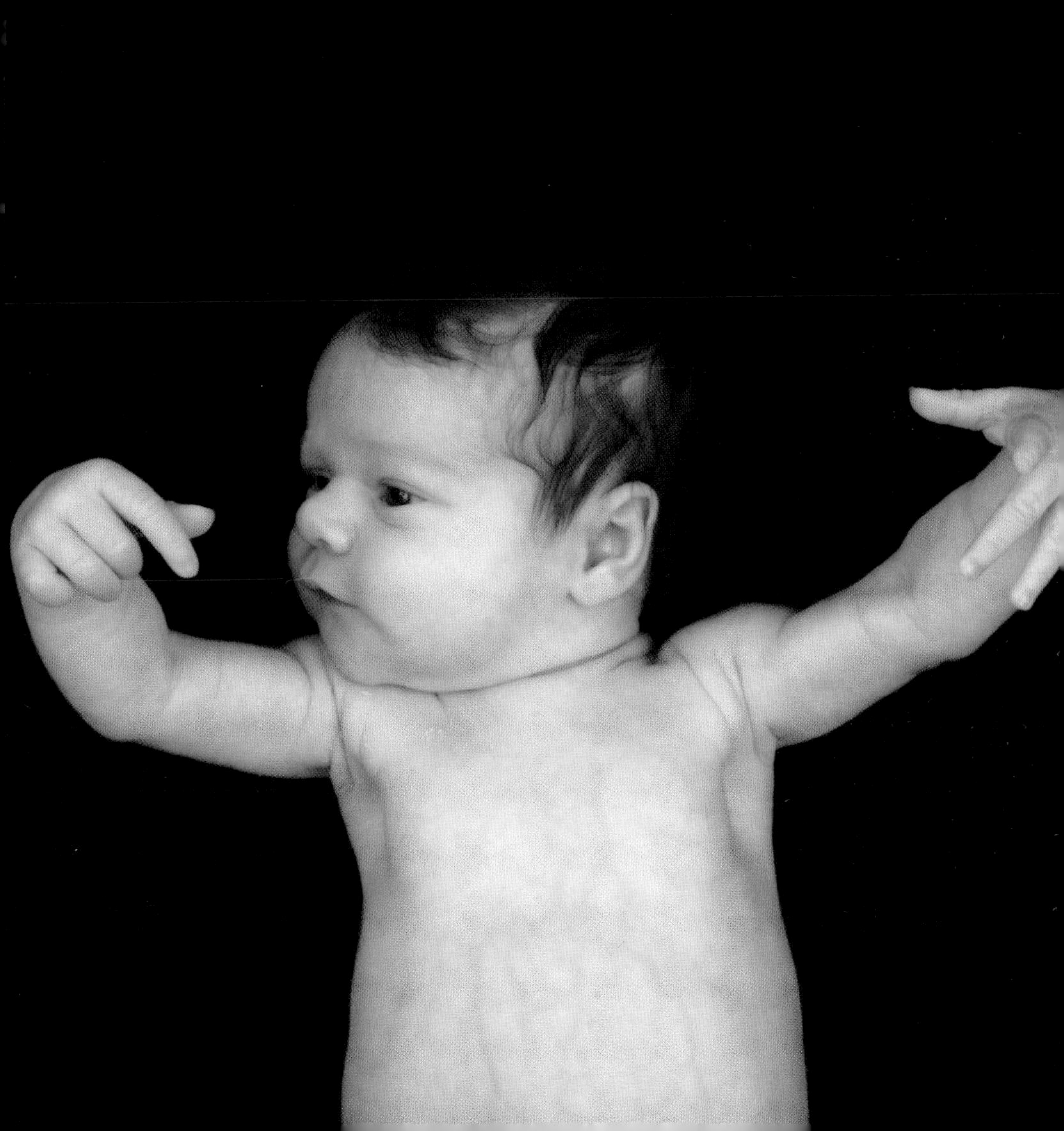

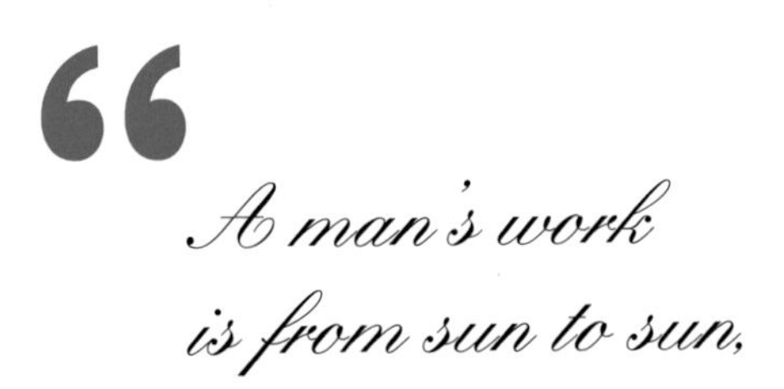

but a mother’s work
is never done. ”

- **UNKNOWN**

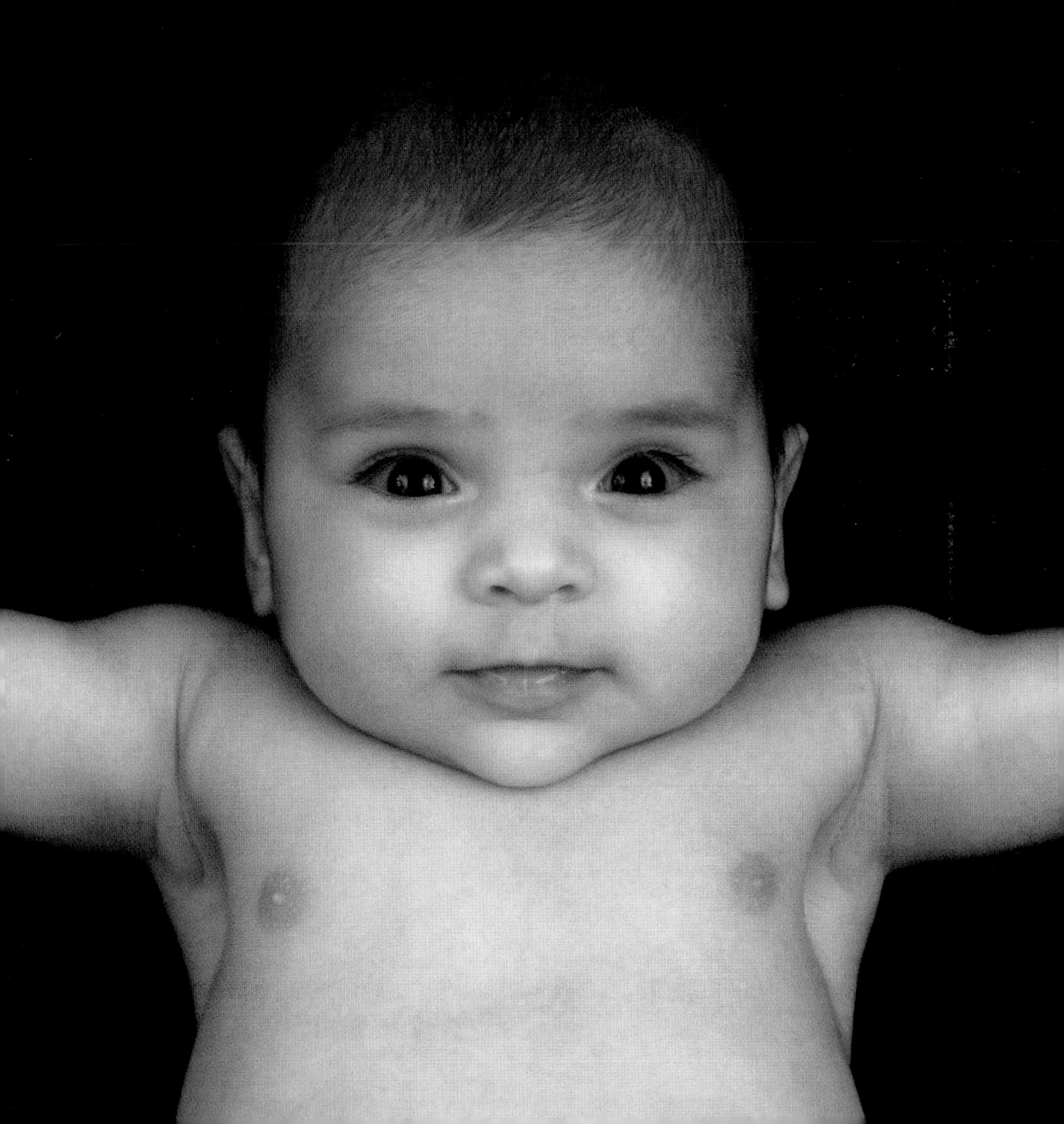

“

Imagine a child with my beauty and your brains.

Yes, but what if the child inherits my beauty and your brains?

”

- ISADORA DUNCAN AND GEORGE BERNARD SHAW

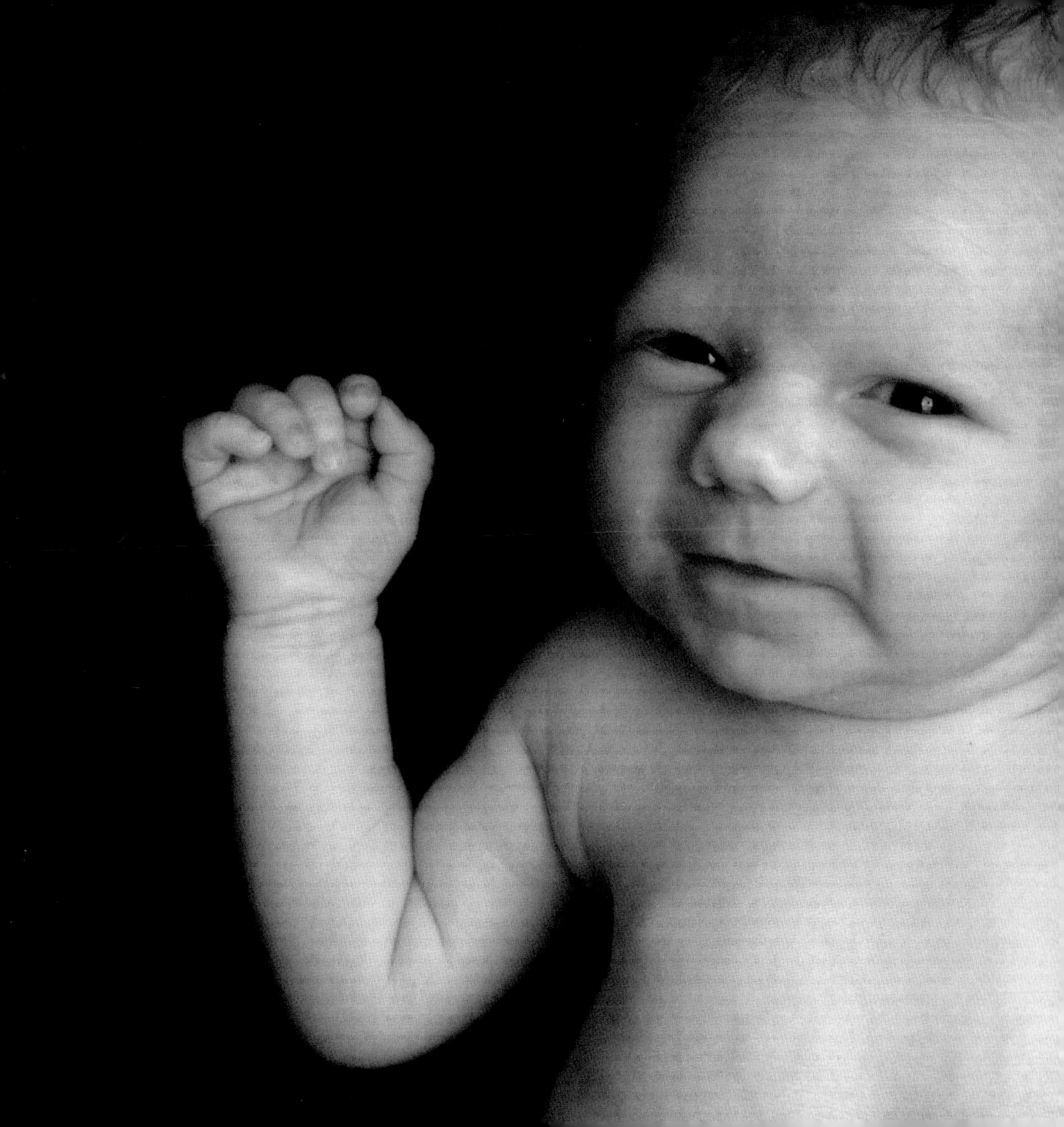

Warning: Remove child before folding

- INSTRUCTIONS ON PUSHCHAIR

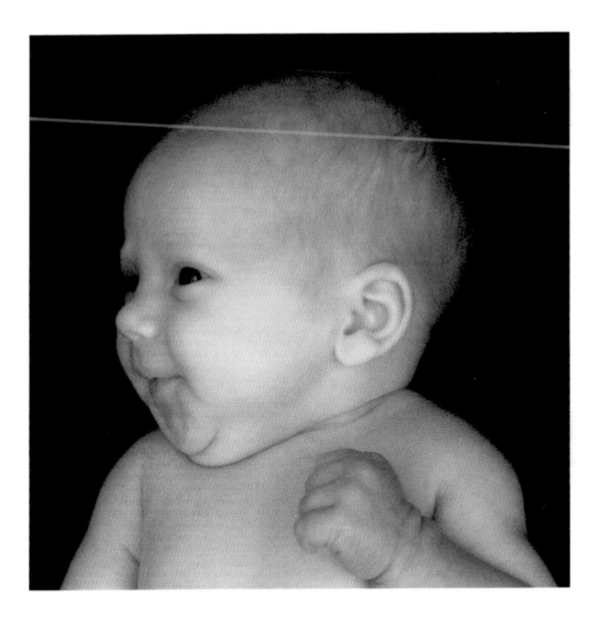

“

Always kiss your children goodnight

- even if they are already asleep.

”

- H. JACKSON BROWN JR.

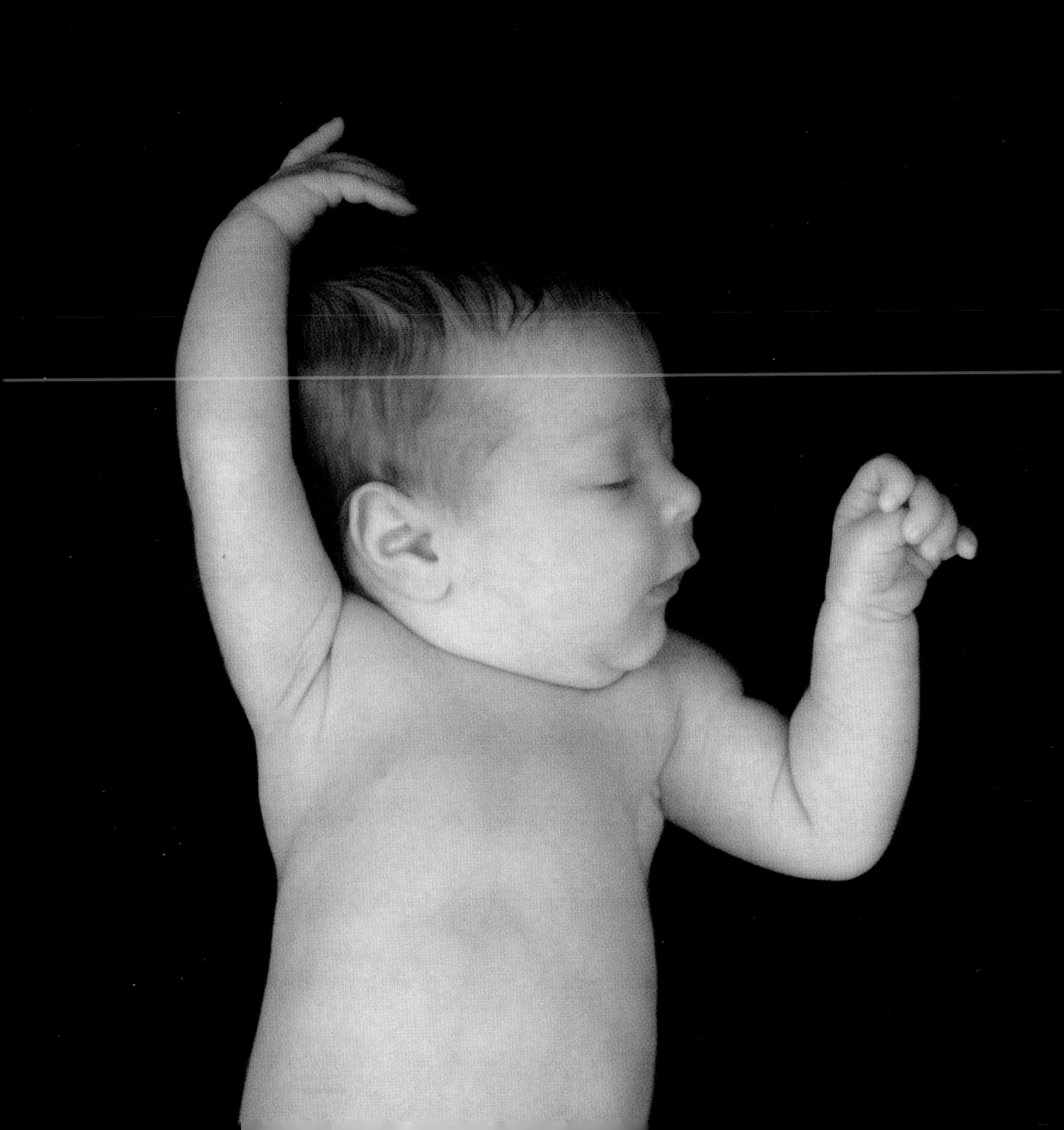